PEOPLE MAGNET: CRACK THE CODE TO CHARISMA

How To Be Interesting, Confident And Charming In Any Situation, Even If You're An Introvert

RACHEL STONE

Copyright © 2023 by Rachel Stone

All rights reserved.

No part of this book may be reproduced in any form or by any electronic or mechanical means, including information storage and retrieval systems, without written permission from the author, except for the use of brief quotations in a book review.

Contents

Introduction ... ix
The Importance Of Being Interesting ... xi

1. UNRAVELLING THE MYSTERY BEHIND INTERESTING PEOPLE: ... 1
Most common questions and answers about being interesting ... 2
Myths and truths about interesting people ... 4
Famous interesting people and why they are interesting ... 7
Key traits that make people interesting and how you can develop them ... 8
The habits of interesting people that you can adopt in your own life ... 10

2. THE NEW YOU: THE MINDSET OF AN INTERESTING PERSON ... 14
Most common questions and answers about mindset ... 15
The power of positive thinking and how it can make you more interesting ... 17
Thought patterns and beliefs that make someone interesting and captivating ... 19
How to shift your mindset to become more curious, open-minded, and engaging in conversations ... 21
How to embrace your unique qualities and use them to your advantage ... 22
Practical tips for overcoming social anxiety and shyness ... 23
How to attract and connect with like-minded individuals who appreciate your unique perspective ... 25
Telling your tale and sharing experiences ... 26
Being an attentive listener ... 26

3. MASTERING THE ART OF STORYTELLING ... 28
Most common questions and answers around storytelling ... 29
Myths and truths around storytelling ... 31

Discover the power of storytelling to engage people emotionally	33
Discover the essential elements of an engaging story and how to structure it for maximum impact	34
Practical techniques for engaging your audience through storytelling	34
Develop your unique storytelling style and voice	35

4. DEVELOPING YOUR INTERESTS — 37

Most common questions and answers about developing your interests	38
Myths and truths about developing your interests	39
Explore your passions and understand why they make you interesting	41
Establish a growth mindset that encourages exploration and learning	43

5. EXPANDING YOUR COMFORT ZONE — 46

Most common questions and answers about expanding your comfort zone	47
Myths and truths regarding expanding your comfort zone	48
Understanding the importance of risk-taking	50
Why does embracing change help make me a people magnet?	51
What are your gains from confronting your fears?	52
Understanding the importance of stepping outside your comfort zone and why it leads to personal development	53
Discover effective methods for overcoming anxiety when engaging in new activities	54
Develop resilience and adaptability in the face of uncertainty and change	55
Why doesn't everybody intentionally try to be resilient?	56
Discover practical techniques for overcoming fear and anxiety when trying new things	58
Stay curious	61
Discover how expanding your comfort zone can lead to new opportunities and experiences	62
Overcoming social anxiety	63

6. BUILDING CONFIDENCE — 65

Most common questions and answers about building confidence	66
Myths and truths about building confidence	68
How to develop a strong sense of self and why it is necessary	69
Understanding the importance of confidence for building relationships and achieving success	72
Practical techniques for conquering self-doubt	73
Discovering how confidence can increase interest and engagement	74
How to become assertive	75
Your personal brand	76
7. ENHANCING YOUR SOCIAL SKILLS	**79**
The two most commonly asked questions about social skills	80
Myths and truths about social skills	80
Building rapport and making an impressive first impression	84
Fostering confidence and self-assurance to navigate social situations with ease	86
Handling difficult conversations and conflict resolution	87
Discovering how to network effectively and establish long-lasting relationships	89
Enhancing emotional intelligence and self-awareness	90
Gaining an understanding of cultural differences and communicating effectively with people of diverse backgrounds	91
8. TRAVELLING AND CULTIVATING EXPERIENCES	**94**
Most common questions and answers about travel	95
Myths and truths about travelling	97
Fears around doing this before and how to overcome them	98
The benefits of travel for you and your self-esteem	100
Understand the importance of travel and new experiences in personal growth and development	102
Practical techniques for travel planning and budgeting	104
Immersing yourself in local culture	106

Develop a sense of curiosity and wonder that can enhance your appreciation for life	108
Cultivating experiences in your daily life, even if you can't travel	110
Discover how to communicate your experiences effectively to others, which can make you more interesting	111
How to build a network of like-minded travellers	112

9. FINDING YOUR VOICE — 115

Most common questions and answers about finding your voice	116
Myths and truths about finding your voice	117
The importance of speaking up	118
How to express yourself confidently	119
The importance of finding your voice in personal and professional development	120
Practical techniques for identifying your values, beliefs, and passions	121
How to stand out and make a difference with what you have to say	122
Gain the confidence to share your voice in personal and professional settings	123
How to navigate challenges and setbacks when expressing your voice	124

10. THE POWER OF EMBRACING CHALLENGES — 126

Most common questions and answers about embracing challenges	127
Myths and truths regarding embracing challenges	129
Gaining confidence in your ability to tackle difficult situations	130

11. THE POWER OF NETWORKING — 133

Most common questions and answers regarding networking	134
Myths and truths about the art of networking	137
Developing the skills to communicate your personal brand and value proposition	140
How to leverage your network to create opportunities	141
The psychology of networking - how to make a memorable impression	143

How to be unforgettable	146
12. A-Z GLOSSARY OF TERMS	149

Introduction

Welcome to **'People Magnet: Crack The Code To Charisma',** a book designed to revolutionise how you approach social interactions, network at events, and build relationships.

Are you having difficulty making connections or being the centre of attention during social gatherings? Perhaps lacking charisma and confidence is making your life difficult. If that describes you, then this book is exactly what's needed!

'People Magnet' will teach you the art of charismatic leadership, including strategies on how to cultivate qualities that draw others naturally to you. Whether you're introverted or extroverted, this book will enable you to unlock your full potential so that you become the life of any party or group meeting, as well as an experienced professional with peers who respect you in the workplace.

By following a few straightforward steps laid out in this book, you'll learn how to develop a magnetic personality, establish rapport with anyone, and form lasting connections that can benefit you both personally and professionally. By doing this, you'll discover how to

Introduction

overcome shyness, anxiety, and fears of rejection, and instead embrace your unique qualities and utilise them effectively.

'People Magnet' is more than just a book on social skills. It provides a roadmap to living a full and satisfying life through meaningful relationships. By applying its principles, this book can help you build an ecosystem of supportive friends and colleagues to help you achieve your goals and make life more fulfilling than ever.

As the author of **'People Magnet'**, my goal is to share my experiences and knowledge of what it takes to be a charismatic person. After experiencing my own difficulties with social anxiety and shyness firsthand, I understand the challenge it presents when trying to engage others, yet with the proper mindset and approaches, anyone can develop confidence and charisma and become a true people magnet.

No matter if you are a student, professional, or simply someone looking to increase your social skills, I invite you to join me on this journey to unlock your full potential and become who God intended you to be.

Let's begin, shall we?

The Importance Of Being Interesting

Being engaging as a person can have a positive influence on all areas of our lives, including our emotional, sexual, financial, and mental well-being.

Here are some examples of how:

Emotionally: Being interesting can open the door to more meaningful relationships, increasing our feelings of happiness and fulfilment within relationships. Engaging conversations that highlight unique perspectives create emotional bonds between us that strengthen interactions between people.

Sexual: Being captivating makes us more desirable to potential partners. With an engaging personality, we exude confidence and charisma that make us more desirable in relationships, adding excitement and novelty that contribute to both sexual and emotional satisfaction for both partners.

Financial: Being an engaging individual can also have financial advantages, such as drawing in new business deals and opportunities, networking and building new connections, and expanding job possibilities. People with unique perspectives, ideas, and solutions are highly valued within professional environments, resulting in higher salaries and greater financial success.

Mental: Curiosity can also play an essential role in our mental health. With an inquisitive spirit and mind, we often seek new experiences and challenges that allow us to grow and learn. Taking part in mentally stimulating activities may help keep the brain sharp while lowering the risk of cognitive decline as we age.

The opposite of interesting

Dull or uninteresting conversations and topics can leave both participants feeling bored, disconnected, and disengaged. Without engaging with what's being discussed or written about in-depth, it can become challenging to stay engaged while remaining attentive, often leading to thoughts wandering or restlessness in both parties involved.

As with conversations that lack stimulation or appeal, speaking with uninteresting individuals can leave us feeling disengaged from the conversation and disassociated from each other, making it harder for us to form meaningful bonds and solid relationships.

Being fascinating can make both you and others feel energised, engaged, and connected. By showing genuine interest in whatever conversation or topic is at hand, it is more likely that you will remain attentive while feeling passionately excited to discuss the issue at hand.

As you talk with someone interesting, you may feel more engaged with the conversation and can form deeper ties based on shared passions and interests. This can lead to longer and stronger relationships being formed with someone special.

Cultivating an intriguing mindset can help you stand out from the competition and leave an indelible mark on those around you. By accepting yourself for what makes you unique and honing your conversational skills, you can become someone people look forward to spending time with and conversing with.

Establishing an interesting mindset is difficult because it involves altering perspective and cultivating new habits and skills. Some have attempted to become more interesting by mimicking others or trying to fit into certain moulds, but such strategies often fall short because they are non-authentic or do not provide lasting solutions.

One reason it's challenging to maintain an interesting mindset is that you have to step outside your comfort zone and take risks; this may feel unnerving and challenging if you are shy or introverted. Cultivating such an interesting state requires a commitment to lifelong learning and personal growth over time, which may become challenging.

Many have tried to become more interesting by trying to impress others with their accomplishments or knowledge, yet this approach often backfires and comes across as arrogant or inauthentic. To truly cultivate an engaging mindset, it's vitally important that people foster authentic curiosity for learning and discovery through genuine exploration.

An often-made mistake when trying to become more interesting is to limit the focus solely on external appearance or social status. While these aspects of being interesting are certainly influential, they're not the sole contributors. If you truly want to stand out from the crowd, you must cultivate unique perspectives, awareness, and authenticity within yourself. You need to work on building up the self-awareness and authenticity that make someone interesting.

The Importance Of Being Interesting

Attaining an intriguing mindset involves being willing to accept yourself for who you are while continually developing skills and habits that reflect those unique to you. Focusing on personal growth and genuine curiosity will allow you to cultivate an intriguing yet authentic attitude, leaving a lasting impression on those around you.

To become more interesting, it is necessary to cultivate an engaging mindset by accepting yourself for who you are, honing your skills and habits, embracing personal development opportunities, and developing genuine curiosity about others. Shifting perspectives, practising positive thinking, and understanding the unique attributes that make someone interesting are all necessary steps for embracing oneself as well as overcoming social anxiety or shyness. You can meet like-minded individuals by attending events, sharing your story, and volunteering for causes or organisations that align with your values and interests. Through personal growth and authenticity, you can become someone others enjoy talking to and being around, leaving a lasting impression on those you encounter along the way.

Why being an interesting person will benefit you

Being more interesting can bring many advantages to your life. Here are a few clear and not-so-obvious ways that embracing an intriguing mindset could enrich it:

Attract others: As an interesting person, you are more likely to attract like-minded individuals and form meaningful connections with them, which leads to increased social support, greater happiness, and an overall more fulfilling social life.

Career opportunities: Maintaining an appealing mindset in professional settings can increase the odds of landing new job opportunities or promotions, and can even help you think creatively and solve workplace problems more efficiently.

Personal growth: Cultivating an engaging mindset requires dedicating yourself to personal development and lifelong learning, leading to greater self-awareness, increased confidence, and a greater sense of purpose and fulfilment in life.

Enhance your creativity: Adopting an engaging mindset can foster creativity and challenge you to think outside the box. By accepting and celebrating your unique qualities and perspective, you may discover new concepts or create works of art or literature.

An increased sense of adventure: An engaging mindset can encourage you to try new experiences, whether that means travelling to foreign lands, trying unfamiliar foods, or learning a new skill. Having such an open mindset allows you to embrace challenges as opportunities.

Greater sense of purpose: By cultivating an engaging mindset and following your passions, you can develop a greater sense of purpose in life and prioritise goals and values more efficiently, leading to a fulfilling, purpose-driven existence.

1

Unravelling The Mystery Behind Interesting People:
HOW TO BECOME ONE YOURSELF

Have you been impressed by someone whose charisma effortlessly captivates all those around them?

In this chapter, we'll unpack what makes these people so compelling and I will provide practical strategies on how you can become like one of them.

First, we will address frequently asked questions and dispel the myths about interesting people. Next, we will explore famous figures who are considered intriguing as well as the key characteristics that set them apart. Finally, we will look at studies conducted on interesting individuals to gain in-depth knowledge of them.

From improving conversational skills to adopting customs that make you more engaging, this chapter will help you create a dynamic and captivating personality. Not only will you gain knowledge on how to be more interesting, but you will also learn how to build stronger relationships and leave lasting impressions on all those you meet!

Are you ready to discover how fascinating people work and

become one yourself? First, let's answer some of the most common questions about unravelling the mystery of becoming interesting.

Most common questions and answers about being interesting

Here are the answers to some of the most frequently asked questions and their respective answers on becoming an interesting person:

Q: Can anyone become interesting, or is charisma only reserved for people born with it?

A: Anyone can become interesting over time with hard work and application. Although some individuals may possess natural charismatic tendencies that give them an advantage, being interesting doesn't solely depend on genetics.

Q: What are some key traits of interesting people?

A: Authenticity, creativity, curiosity, empathy, and having a growth mindset are hallmarks of interestingness in people.

Q: How can I develop these traits to become more interesting?

A: Mastering these skills takes time and effort. Some ways of cultivating them include exploring your passions and interests, seeking new experiences, practising active listening techniques, and cultivating positive thinking patterns.

Q: To be interesting, do I have to be outgoing and extroverted?

A: Being outgoing is not necessary to be interesting; introverts can also make themselves interesting by connecting meaningfully with people and sharing their unique viewpoints.

Q: How can I enhance my conversational skills to become more engaging and interesting?

A: To develop stronger conversational abilities, practise active listening, pose thoughtful questions, and share your unique viewpoints and experiences, which can all help make conversations more interesting and captivating.

Q: Will being vulnerable make me more interesting?

A: Absolutely. Being open about your struggles and difficulties makes you more relatable and human, and therefore more interesting!

Q: What are some characteristics of interesting people I can emulate?

A: Traits common among interesting individuals include seeking new experiences, staying curious, following their passions, and maintaining a positive attitude.

Q: Will travelling make me a more interesting person?

A: Absolutely. Travel can offer new experiences and perspectives that can enhance your appeal to others, making you even more captivating to them.

Q: Will becoming an interesting person help my personal and professional life?

A: Yes, it will. Being interesting can help build stronger relationships and leave an everlasting impression on those you meet, which is invaluable both personally and professionally.

Q: How long will it take me to become an interesting person?

A: Becoming interesting takes effort over time; no set timeline exists as each journey differs for every individual.

Myths and truths about interesting people

Myth: Interesting people are born that way.

Truth: While certain individuals may possess an innate capacity for being interesting, being so isn't solely determined by genetics.

Anyone can develop the traits associated with being interesting through application and effort.

Myth: Interesting people tend to be outgoing and outspoken.

Truth: Being an extrovert makes engaging with other people easier, but introverts can still be captivating individuals if they know how to connect with people in meaningful ways.

Myth: Engaging lives full of adventure are synonymous with interesting lives.

Truth: Though interesting people may have more thrilling or exotic experiences, what often makes them compelling are their perspectives and how they share them with others.

Myth: Interesting people must be popular and liked by everyone.

Truth: No matter how appealing someone may appear, despite their value system or interests, what makes an interesting individual worth keeping an eye out for is often their uniqueness as individuals while creating meaningful connections with like-minded individuals who share similar ideals and goals.

Myth: Interesting people don't get bored.

Truth: Even interesting people experience boredom from time to time; however, their curiosity typically leads them to seek new experiences and challenges.

Myth Interesting people must always be the centre of attention.

Truth: While interesting people may possess natural charisma that draws people towards them, this doesn't cause them to be at the centre of attention all the time. Interesting individuals make others feel seen and heard, even in group settings.

Myth: Engaging individuals are always positive and content.

Truth: Interesting, engaging people experience emotions too. What makes them fascinating usually lies in their ability to manage and express these emotions.

Myth: Interesting people always know what to say.

Truth: Nobody always knows exactly what to say, including interesting people. However, those with strong listening skills and the capacity for thoughtful responses usually show this characteristic more readily than most others.

Myth: Engaging individuals must be wealthy and successful.

Truth: While financial success can certainly be impressive, being fascinating does not depend on this. Instead, interesting people often have passions beyond financial gain that they engagingly share with others.

Myth: Interesting people don't have any flaws or insecurities.

Truth: Everyone has flaws and insecurities, including those considered interesting. What makes them interesting, however, is often their willingness to open up about themselves and share their struggles openly, making them relatable and human in the eyes of others.

Famous interesting people and why they are interesting

Here are a few notable and interesting people and what makes them so appealing:

Elon Musk has long been revered as an innovator and futurist. Through Tesla and SpaceX, his ground-breaking ideas and futuristic vision have revolutionised the automotive and space industries. His commitment to making our planet better through sustainable technology makes him an inspiring figure to many people.

Ruth Bader Ginsburg: As the second female justice ever appointed to the United States Supreme Court, Ginsburg made history for women's rights and equality. Her intelligence, determination, and commitment to justice made her one of America's greatest figures.

David Bowie was one of the most ground-breaking musicians of his time and an influential cultural icon, known for his fearless creativity and innovative musical style. Bowie inspired artists and fans alike through his ability to reinvent himself over time and push musical boundaries forward.

Malala Yousafzai: Malala Yousafzai has earned both international renown and praise as a Nobel Peace Prize laureate and advocate for education and women's rights, distinguished by her bravery and resilience under pressure. Her unflinching commitment to her beliefs and determination to make a change has made her an inspirational figure whom many look up to as a role model.

Oprah Winfrey has become an iconic figure worldwide as a media mogul, philanthropist, and advocate for self-improvement. Her ability to connect with people and inspire positive change has cemented her place as one of the world's premier figures in her field. Her dedication to personal development and empowerment has cemented this status for millions worldwide.

What makes these individuals truly remarkable is their ability to pursue their passions and create meaningful change within their respective fields. Their distinct perspectives, innovative ideas, and unfaltering devotion to their beliefs have rendered them both captivating and inspirational to many people around them.

Key traits that make people interesting and how you can develop them

Here are a few traits that distinguish individuals as engaging and ways to develop them:

Authenticity: Being true and genuine are hallmarks of engaging people. To foster authenticity, focus on being honest about who you are rather than conforming to external expectations.

Creativity: Thinking outside the box and expressing oneself creatively are important parts of being interesting. To foster your creativity, experiment with different mediums and challenge yourself to think unconventionally.

Curiosity: An open and curious mindset can open the door to many exciting experiences and insights. To develop it, ask questions, seek new information and experiences, and keep an open mind.

Empathy: Being able to understand and connect with others' emotions and perspectives is the cornerstone of successful interpersonal interactions and dialogues. To foster empathy, actively listen and try seeing things from different points of view.

A mindset of growth and development: Acknowledging the possibility of development can bring many rewarding experiences and personal growth. To develop this attitude, embrace challenges as opportunities to learn more about yourself and look out for new experiences and perspectives.

Humour: Humour can make people more memorable and engaging. To develop yourself, don't take yourself too seriously and look out for absurdities in everyday situations. Try being quick on your feet with quick quips and jokes to connect with people more efficiently.

Individuality: Recognising one's individual qualities and expressing them authentically are two keys to developing individuality. To foster it, celebrate your quirks and interests while discovering your passions. Don't be afraid of standing out!

Listening: Actively listening and showing interest in others' experiences and perspectives is key to building meaningful relationships and finding someone fascinating. To develop listening skills, focus on the speaker while asking relevant questions without interrupting or interjecting your own thoughts.

Mindfulness: Being present and aware of our thoughts and emotions can open doors to incredible insights and self-discovery. To achieve mindfulness, try practising meditation or other mindfulness techniques, taking regular breaks throughout the day to relax, and paying attention to your thoughts and feelings. These activities will all contribute to an increased presence.

Versatility: Being adaptable and versatile in different situations is one key element of being more interesting and capable. To build it, challenge yourself to try new things outside your comfort zone, practise being open-minded, and develop a variety of interests and skills.

The habits of interesting people that you can adopt in your own life

Here are a few habits of interesting people you could adopt in your own life:

Pursue your passions: Engaging individuals often have strong personal goals that drive their decisions forward. To adopt this habit yourself, identify what your passions and interests are and set aside regular time to explore them.

Stay curious: Curious people are constantly in pursuit of new experiences and knowledge. To join their ranks, ask questions, take risks, and remain open-minded.

Try this:

Engage in dialogue: Start asking more questions in your daily interactions to better understand others and delve deeper into topics of interest to you.

Bring new experiences into your life: Be open to trying something different and seek opportunities for discovery, such as new foods, places, or hobbies!

Make an effort to learn something new every day: Make it your daily goal to acquire some new information by reading an article, watching a TED talk, or signing up for an online course.

Acknowledging uncertainty: Instead of fearing uncertainty as an opportunity for growth and learning, embrace it as an invitation to explore something outside your comfort zone that causes anxiety - even if that means starting small!

Engage in conversation: Strive to have engaging and insightful discussions with others by asking probing questions that deepen your understanding of their perspectives and experiences.

Be present: Interesting people tend to be fully present in each moment, taking an interest in what's going on around them. To develop this habit yourself, practise mindfulness and concentrate on being fully immersed in each experience that crosses your path.

Engage challenges: Remarkable people often push themselves beyond their comfort zones to welcome and pursue challenges head-on. If this sounds appealing to you, seek out new challenges, take risks, and view failure as an opportunity for learning.

Connect with others: Engaging individuals are usually great at making meaningful relationships. To form this habit, practise active listening, show genuine interest in others, and build deeper relationships.

Express yourself authentically: Interesting people tend to have unique perspectives and can articulate themselves authentically. To do so yourself, celebrate individualism, communicate honestly about thoughts and emotions, and don't be afraid of standing out from the crowd.

Experience new things: Attractive people tend to seek new experiences and push themselves outside their comfort zones, constantly searching for something different to try, travelling to new places, and challenging themselves to step outside their routine. Make this your goal, and don't settle into a routine!

Things you could try:

Start a new hobby: Try taking up something like painting, dancing, or learning a foreign language, as this will allow you to discover new passions and interests.

Explore a new area: Take a stroll in an unfamiliar neighbourhood, park, or area of town that you haven't been to before and discover new sights, sounds, and experiences. This will lead you down a new path of discovery!

Experience new foods: Visit a restaurant that serves an unfamiliar cuisine to discover different flavours and cultures. Doing this will allow you to open yourself up to new tastes and experiences.

Experience something cultural: Attend an unfamiliar cultural event or festival for the first time, such as a music festival, art show, or exhibition, that can help expand your horizons about different cultures and traditions. This can provide valuable opportunities to gain new perspectives on global issues.

Attend a class: Enrol in a class in an area of interest for which you lack prior experience; perhaps cooking, photography, or learning a foreign language could all qualify as classes that would interest you.

Travel: Planning a trip will allow you to discover new cultures, meet interesting people, and gain insight into various lifestyles.

Read and learn: Remarkable individuals often possess a thirst for knowledge, constantly looking to expand their minds through books, lectures, or any means necessary for personal development. To take up this habit yourself, try reading books, attending lectures, or searching out opportunities to help with this aspect of development.

Focus on gratitude: Remaining optimistic in life requires cultivating gratitude. To do so successfully, take note of all that's good in your life, express your appreciation frequently, and work on cultivating an optimistic outlook.

Above all, engage with others. Successful and popular people are known for being engaged with their work, hobbies, and relationships. To adopt this habit yourself, stay committed to your goals and interests while prioritising relationships and remaining actively involved with whatever activity is at hand.

2

The New You: The Mindset Of An Interesting Person
HOW TO CULTIVATE IT AND STAND OUT FROM THE CROWD

Are you tired of feeling like just another face in the crowd?

Yearning to become someone people want to get to know better and like more? This chapter will equip you with tools and techniques for doing just that.

We will explore the thought processes and beliefs that make someone engaging while teaching you how to shift your own mindset to become more curious, open-minded, and conversational.

Integrating your unique qualities and using them effectively are key components of creating an intriguing mindset, and I will offer practical tips and strategies on how to do just that.

Finally, we will address the importance of confidence in becoming interesting, providing tips to overcome social anxiety and shyness.

By the end of this chapter, you will have a fresh outlook on life and be equipped with techniques for becoming an engaging individual. By making more interesting connections and increasing self-assurance with an interesting mindset, this chapter can help you take your next steps toward personal fulfilment and self-sufficiency.

So let's get going!

Most common questions and answers about mindset

Here are the answers to some of the most frequently asked questions and concerns about developing an engaging mindset:

Q: Is it possible to alter my attitude and become more interesting?

A: Absolutely! Adopting an interesting mindset takes effort but is achievable over time.

Q: To become more interesting, do I have to completely transform my personality?

A: Nope - developing an interesting mindset requires shifting your perspective and adopting new habits.

Q: Can I become more interesting even though I'm naturally introverted or shy?

A: Absolutely - being introverted or shy doesn't rule you out as being interesting. Developing the confidence to share your unique perspective with others and build meaningful relationships is what counts!

Q: Can positive thinking make me more engaging and interesting to be around?

A: Positive thinking can help you approach situations with an open mind, see the good in others, and foster curiosity and wonder. All this makes for more engaging and captivating interactions!

Q: How can I embrace and use my unique qualities effectively?

A: Begin by identifying your personal strengths and passions, then find ways to incorporate them into your daily life. Share your unique perspectives and experiences with others without fear of standing out from the pack.

Q: What are some practical strategies for overcoming social anxiety and shyness?

A: To reduce social anxiety and shyness, start practising active listening, asking thoughtful questions, and paying close attention during conversations. Take small steps outside your comfort zone; challenge negative thought patterns by practising positive affirmation techniques.

Q: Will developing an interesting mindset help in my personal and professional lives?

A: Absolutely! Being engaging can help build stronger relationships, make a lasting impression on people, and open doors of opportunity in both your personal and professional lives.

The power of positive thinking and how it can make you more interesting

Altering your perspective on life can be an effective way to foster an engaging mindset.

Here are a few techniques that may help you change it:

Practise gratitude: Recognising all that's good in your life can help cultivate a more optimistic mindset. Make a point to recognise all the things for which you should be grateful daily and to take time out each day to appreciate even the smallest of things!

Cultivate curiosity: Approach each day with wonder and curiosity. Be open to new experiences and perspectives, asking questions to deepen your understanding of the world around you.

Here are a few questions you can pose to yourself to spark curiosity:

- *What are some things I am curious about but have never explored?*
- *How can I approach this situation from an alternative viewpoint?*
- *What am I taking away from this person or experience that I may not have thought about before?*
- *What are some possible solutions to my current dilemma?*
- *How can I challenge my own assumptions and biases in this situation?*

- *What might happen if I tried something completely out of my comfort zone?*
- *What are some things I don't know, and how can I gain more information about them?*
- *How can I incorporate different perspectives into my thinking and decision-making processes?*
- *Which questions can I pose to gain more in-depth knowledge of this topic or situation?*
- *How can I maintain my sense of wonder and curiosity throughout my daily life?*

Accept uncertainty: Instead of fearing what lies beyond, embrace uncertainty as an opportunity for growth and learning. Step outside your comfort zone and try new things, even if they seem frightening at first. Your world might expand as a result!

Reframe negative thoughts: Whenever negative thoughts emerge, try reframing them in a more positive light. Instead of thinking, *"I'm not good enough,"* try reframing it as, *"I am always learning and progressing forward."*

Mindfulness meditation or other techniques can help. Being present can lead to a greater appreciation of life and more positivity in your outlook. Practise mindfulness meditation or other techniques designed to keep you grounded in the moment.

Positive thinking is a fundamental element of creating an engaging mindset, so here are a few techniques to help cultivate it:

Daily affirmations: Engaging in daily affirmation exercises can help build up a more positive self-image and outlook on life.

Visualise success: Visualising success can help keep you on the path toward achieving your goals and leading a fulfilling life. Doing this can keep you focused and motivated towards the positive outcomes you seek to accomplish.

Surround yourself with positive people: Spending time around supportive individuals can help maintain a positive mindset and avoid negativity.

Focus on solutions instead of problems: When faced with obstacles or setbacks, stay optimistic by finding solutions rather than dwelling on the problem itself. Doing this can help keep you feeling positive and proactive.

By changing your perspective and cultivating a positive outlook on life, you can become a more interesting individual who appreciates everything around them more fully.

Thought patterns and beliefs that make someone interesting and captivating

Here are some patterns and beliefs that make people intriguing and captivating, along with practical steps you can start taking today:

Curiosity: Engaging individuals tend to be naturally curious about the world around them. They ask questions, seek new experiences, and approach life with wonder and awe. To increase curiosity in yourself and others, start asking more questions in daily interactions; seek new experiences such as new foods or activities; make an effort each day to learn something new; and start asking more questions of others too.

Open-mindedness: Engaging individuals are those who welcome new ideas and viewpoints without dismissing those different from themselves or quickly judging others. To build this trait, try actively searching out and listening to various perspectives; engaging with people from diverse backgrounds or beliefs; engaging in conversations about those topics without preconceptions forming; and approaching situations without preconceived notions in mind.

Growth mindset: Intriguing individuals recognise challenges as opportunities for personal growth and aren't afraid of failure; they strive for improvements constantly. To develop this type of perspective, start reframing challenges as opportunities for learning; celebrate your successes while acknowledging failures as lessons to grow from.

Authenticity: Engaging individuals are those who remain true to themselves without trying to be someone they're not, accepting themselves for who they are while not hiding their unique qualities, opinions, and beliefs. To cultivate authenticity, start by identifying your core values and beliefs; express them honestly and openly while daring to stand out.

Passion: Remarkable people usually possess an enduring passion that propels them forward, be it their hobby, interest, or cause. To cultivate passion in yourself, start by identifying your interests and hobbies. Make time regularly to pursue these areas of interest while seeking opportunities to hone them further.

Empathy: People who make you curious tend to be highly empathic and can develop deep connections with others on an intimate level. They know how to put themselves in another person's shoes, showing genuine concern for their well-being and actively listening to others. Listening with empathy will allow you to build it into your everyday interactions! Start building empathy today by actively listening to those around you and trying on different perspectives. Try being kind and compassionate wherever possible in your daily interactions; this will only strengthen it further!

Creativity: Engaging individuals often possess a creative mindset and can think creatively outside the box. They don't shy away from taking risks and are always exploring novel solutions to problems. To cultivate creativity, take time to daydream and imagine new possibilities; accept your unique perspective while exploring unfamiliar experiences; don't be afraid of change or taking chances!

How to shift your mindset to become more curious, open-minded, and engaging in conversations

Here are some strategies for shifting your mindset to become more curious, open-minded, and engaged in conversations:

Challenge your assumptions: Take time to examine and question your beliefs and assumptions, actively look for evidence that supports or opposes them, and build up a more nuanced and open-minded perspective. This exercise could open doors of creativity.

Accept discomfort: Seek out challenging or uncomfortable situations as opportunities to grow and learn from them. For example, attend social events where no one you know will be attending and challenge yourself to strike up conversations with new people.

Play devil's advocate: Adopt an opposing viewpoint during conversations to expand your perspective and spark more engaging, thought-provoking discussions. Doing this may open new avenues of thought.

Focus on active listening: Instead of thinking ahead to what you will say next in a conversation, try listening to what someone else is telling you; this can help you ask more thoughtful questions and have more meaningful discussions.

Explore unfamiliar experiences: Seek out unexpected and innovative experiences outside your comfort zone to develop an open and curious outlook on life. This can help foster more creativity.

Discover different cultures: When travelling and learning about various cultures, taking an in-depth interest in their customs, traditions, and perspectives can open your mind and lead to more interesting conversations among people from diverse backgrounds.

Practise empathy: Put yourself in another's shoes and understand their perspective to form deeper connections and more meaningful conversations with people.

How to embrace your unique qualities and use them to your advantage

Adopting and taking advantage of your unique qualities can be a powerful way to build an interesting mindset and stand out from the crowd.

Here are some practical and innovative steps you can take to embrace them:

Recognising your strengths: Take some time to identify and acknowledge your unique characteristics, list them all out, and think about how you could leverage them in your favour. For example, if you're an amazing storyteller, consider starting a blog or podcast where others can hear about you!

Accept your flaws: Accepting your flaws is just as essential to happiness as accepting your strengths. Accept and work on improving any weaknesses you might have while accepting them as part of what makes you unique. For instance, if you're shyer than most, focus on building deeper connections within smaller groups rather than trying to be the centre of attention at parties!

Discover your niche: Focus on developing skills and expertise in areas you're truly passionate about and become known for them. For instance, if green living is something you are particularly knowledgeable about, consider becoming an expert in it by sharing this information with others.

Being yourself: Don't try to be someone you aren't simply to fit in or impress others; embrace your unique qualities and express them authentically. Don't shy away from showing who you really are—even if that means showing some quirky or eccentric traits, such as humour! Let your unique qualities show.

Surround yourself with supportive people: Surround yourself with people who appreciate and encourage your individual qualities, whether that means finding people who share similar passions and values as yourself or simply being open-minded enough to venture outside your comfort zone and meet new people.

Be bold: Don't be scared to take calculated risks and try new things! Acknowledging your unique qualities often requires venturing outside your comfort zone and taking chances. For example, if starting your own business has always been on your bucket list, why not make this year the year you take that leap and pursue it with gusto?

Practise self-compassion: Be kind and caring towards yourself even when things do not go according to plan. Remember that your unique qualities make you special and valuable, and welcome them as part of your personal journey. For instance, when making mistakes or experiencing setbacks occurs, practise self-compassion by acknowledging feelings while considering how the experience can teach or shape you for future opportunities.

Practical tips for overcoming social anxiety and shyness

Escaping social anxiety and shyness can be daunting, but with a bit of persistence, it's possible to become more comfortable in social settings.

Here are some practical strategies and examples for conquering social anxiety and shyness:

Start small: Challenge yourself to engage in small talk with strangers in low-pressure environments such as waiting in line or visiting a cafe, asking them questions like, *"Which menu item do you recommend?"* and *"Any exciting plans for the weekend?"* to make small talk easier and open doors into dialogue.

Practise active listening: Instead of worrying about what to say next, practise active listening by asking open-ended questions that focus on their answers and then following up with additional follow-up questions based on those responses. For instance, if someone mentions they're taking a vacation, you could ask, *"Where are you headed and what plans do you have in place?"*

Use positive self-talk: Instead of dwelling on your fears and insecurities, try positive self-talk to build up your confidence. Remind yourself that everyone experiences nervousness or anxiety from time to time.

Prepare conversation topics in advance: Before attending a social event, plan out some discussion topics in advance. Consider subjects or current events that interest you or could spark dialogue; for instance, bringing up recent movies you watched or asking for book recommendations are two good ways of engaging others in conversations.

Join groups or clubs: Belonging to a group that shares your interests is an excellent way to meet like-minded individuals and overcome social anxiety. For example, if hiking is something you enjoy doing in your area, why not look into joining a hiking club?

Take deep breaths: When feeling anxious or nervous, try taking some deep breaths to help soothe your nerves. Inhale slowly through your nose while exhaling through your mouth. This technique may work better if used at times when anxiety or nerves flare up.

Practise makes perfect: The more often you engage with social situations, the more comfortable you'll become in social settings. Challenge yourself to engage with people regularly; don't judge yourself harshly if, initially, you feel nervous or shy; social skills can be learned with time and dedication!

How to attract and connect with like-minded individuals who appreciate your unique perspective

Attracting and connecting with individuals who share your unique perspective can be an excellent way to foster an engaging mindset and form meaningful relationships.

Here are some effective methods for finding like-minded individuals:

Recognising your core values and interests: Take some time to identify your core values and interests, as well as the groups and communities that align with them. This can help you form connections with individuals who share similar perspectives.

Attend events and meetups: It can be helpful to attend events and meetups that align with your interests and values, to meet like-minded people and participate in conversations that appreciate your unique perspectives. This can lead to new friendships being formed.

Engage with online communities: Engage with online communities that match your interests and values, to meet like-minded individuals from around the world while sharing your unique perspective with them.

Be genuine: Avoid being someone you aren't to fit in or impress others; embrace your individual qualities and express them authentically to attract individuals who appreciate and value your perspective.

Telling your tale and sharing experiences

Start by reflecting on your journey and noting key moments or experiences that have had an effect on shaping your perspective and values.

Share your story with friends or family members, and observe their reactions and responses carefully. Be open and honest in your storytelling, sharing the highs and lows of your experiences.

Search out opportunities to share your stories in social settings, such as conversations with new acquaintances or group meetings. Engage in active listening and pose inquiries to expand our knowledge about others' experiences and perspectives.

Being an attentive listener

Concentrate on nonverbal cues such as eye contact and body language to demonstrate interest and engagement. Use open-ended questions to encourage others to share their experiences and perspectives. Avoid interrupting or dominating the discussion, and allow others the space to share their views and emotions.

Practise reflective listening by summarising what someone has shared and showing empathy or understanding.

Apply active listening skills both personally and professionally to build trust and rapport and deepen connections with those you meet.

Volunteer for causes or organisations that align with your values and interests to meet like-minded people while having an impactful presence in your community. Doing this will allow you to meet like-minded individuals while making a lasting difference!

Building meaningful relationships takes time and dedication; be patient, remain true to yourself, and engage with people who value your unique perspective.

By changing our mindsets, sharing stories and experiences, and actively listening to others around us, we can become more engaging people while building meaningful connections that last a lifetime.

3

Mastering The Art Of Storytelling
HOW TO CAPTIVATE AND INSPIRE YOUR AUDIENCE

Do you ever find yourself asking why some people seem to be natural storytellers, captivating their audience effortlessly, while others struggle? Or have you come across myths surrounding storytelling, such as whether it is an inherent talent or not?

In this chapter, we'll examine the power of storytelling and how you can master the art of telling compelling tales. We will address frequently asked questions, dispel myths, and discuss what could happen if we fail to harness its immense potential.

Stories are an integral component of social interaction, providing us with a means to connect emotionally with people. They have long been used for entertainment, education, and inspiration. - By understanding what makes a compelling narrative and structuring it effectively, you can engage your audience while communicating complex information more easily.

No matter your background—business professional, public speaker, or anyone looking to build deeper relationships—storytelling provides powerful ways of creating stronger bonds through more engaging interactions. This chapter gives you tools for doing just that!

We will discover how to craft captivating stories, tips for engaging audiences, and the importance of emphasising benefits, solutions, and outcomes rather than emotions when telling our tales.

Get ready to expand your storytelling abilities!

Most common questions and answers around storytelling

Q: How can I become a better storyteller?

A: To become an effective storyteller, practise regularly and pay close attention to how your stories are received by audiences. Make note of which are more engaging or effective, and then work to refine the delivery and pacing of those stories that do well.

Q: What are some common mistakes to avoid when telling a story?

A: Common errors include rambling off on unrelated tangents, losing audience interest, or failing to communicate an obvious moral or message. Furthermore, it's essential not to appear too robotic when speaking; otherwise, this can come across as insincere and disingenuous.

Q: How can I choose the appropriate story?

A: Choose a narrative that is pertinent to the conversation or situation at hand, considering audience preferences and interests. Furthermore, be sure to choose something you care deeply about that you can deliver effectively—something authentic.

Q: How do I engage the audience?

A: Engage your audience when telling a story by using vivid sensory details, speaking enthusiastically and energetically, inviting audience participation by asking questions or inviting participation, and using pauses and tone variations for suspense-building purposes, as well as pausing before speaking again or switching the tone mid-sentence. These techniques should keep their interest peaked and your narrative flowing smoothly.

Q: How long should a story be?

A: The length of any given tale depends upon both its context and target audience. As a general guideline, however, stories should remain concise while providing enough detail for their listener's imagination to create vivid pictures in his or her mind.

Q: How can I convey emotion effectively in my storytelling?

A: An effective way of conveying emotion in storytelling is by using descriptive language, altering your tone of voice, and emphasising key points using body language. Furthermore, being genuine and authentic when speaking will enable your audience to connect on an emotional level with you, and vice versa.

Myths and truths around storytelling

Here are some myths and truths related to being an effective storyteller:

Myth: Being an effective storyteller requires being born with talent.

Truth: Although some individuals may possess natural storytelling talents, developing this skill requires dedication and effort from everyone involved.

Myth: The more elaborate the story is, the better it will be received by listeners.

Truth: Length isn't everything when it comes to storytelling; an engaging narrative can just as effectively deliver its message in just a few sentences as long ones can.

Myth: An effective storyteller always presents himself or herself confidently and without reservation.

Truth: An effective storyteller must be genuine and authentic, showing emotion or vulnerability during the delivery of their story. If pauses or stumbles over words improve storytelling efficiency, then that should be considered acceptable behaviour by storytellers.

Myth: To be an engaging storyteller, a good raconteur must lead an interesting or fulfilling life.

Truth: Though personal experiences make for compelling storytelling material, an effective storyteller can draw inspiration from multiple sources, including books, movies, and the experiences of others.

Myth: For an engaging story to be successful, an effective storyteller must strictly stick to facts.

Truth: An engaging storyteller will often use creative licence with their storytelling to add flair and increase impact while remaining faithful to the message at its core.

Myth: Audience response is the cornerstone of storytelling.

Truth: At the core of storytelling lies its message, or moral. A good storyteller should strive to deliver this message clearly and effectively, regardless of the audience's reaction.

Human beings have been telling stories for millennia. Stories serve to entertain, teach, inspire, and emotionally connect us with one another; from campfire tales to bedtime tales, storytelling plays an essential part in our lives.

Why are stories important in social interactions? The reason lies within them—stories are an effective way of building connections and relationships with others. Listening to another's tale engages, excites, and empathises us; we see things from their point of view while experiencing what their emotions may be like too.

Storytelling can also serve to overcome barriers and foster interpersonal connections. By sharing our narratives with one another and learning from their experiences, storytelling helps bridge divisions between us in today's increasingly interdependent and diverse globalised society.

Discover the power of storytelling to engage people emotionally

At its core, storytelling is about connecting emotionally with people. When we share our tales with others, they experience similar feelings, creating empathy and an understanding between one person and another, which fosters strong bonds between us all.

Storytelling's power lies in its ability to stir emotions and provide an unforgettable shared experience. When we hear an engaging tale that touches us deeply, we feel an immediate connection with its author, perhaps feeling inspired, motivated, or comforted that someone else has experienced something similar.

Understanding the power of storytelling requires acknowledging that emotions are the cornerstone of all meaningful connections with others. By telling our tales in a manner that stirs these powerful feelings within an audience, we can form powerful bonds that last beyond a single telling session.

Discover the essential elements of an engaging story and how to structure it for maximum impact

To tell an engaging tale, it's essential to comprehend all of the components that comprise an excellent narrative. These components include:

Character: To successfully craft an engaging story, one needs a character that resonates with its target audience and that they can relate to.

Conflict: To create an engaging story, every plotline needs a conflict that the protagonist must overcome to progress forward.

Resolution: When dealing with conflicts, the resolution should be in a manner that satisfies both audience members and characters alike.

A great story should have an obvious takeaway message or moral for its readers to understand and internalise.

Once you understand the elements that define a great tale, you can craft your story to have maximum impact. This may involve creating an engaging opening that hooks your audience, developing suspense throughout, and concluding with an uplifting conclusion.

Practical techniques for engaging your audience through storytelling

To engage your audience through storytelling, it's essential to use techniques that capture their interest and keep them involved. These may include:

- Utilising sensory details to paint an emotional picture for the listener.
- Speaking with energy and enthusiasm that will convey your enthusiasm for the story you are sharing.
- Engaging participants by asking questions or seeking feedback.
- Use pauses and tonal shifts to build suspense and keep audiences engaged.
- Focusing on benefits, solutions, and outcomes as well as feelings helps create an engaging narrative.

Using these techniques, you can capture your audience's interest and create an unforgettable storytelling experience.

Develop your unique storytelling style and voice

Every storyteller has their own distinctive style and voice. To develop yours, it is important to experiment with various techniques until you find what works for you. This could include:

- Practising regularly to hone your skills and gain confidence.
- Learning from other storytellers.
- Being authentic and genuine when delivering.
- Being open and willing to accept feedback as a means to enhance your storytelling. Be flexible enough to implement changes that could strengthen it.

Do not underestimate the power of storytelling to foster more engaging, authentic, and meaningful interactions with those around us. Doing this will enable us to motivate, inspire, and connect more closely with those we encounter for a more empathetic and compassionate world.

RACHEL STONE

4

Developing Your Interests
HOW TO DISCOVER YOUR PASSIONS AND ENRICH YOUR LIFE

In this chapter, we'll explore the benefits and outcomes of following your passions as well as dispel myths surrounding this topic. By learning practical techniques for identifying passions and exploring hobbies that interest you, you'll cultivate an open mindset towards learning and experimentation that fosters confidence when sharing interests with others.

Find time for yourself even with a busy schedule by making time for your interests, connecting with like-minded individuals who share them, and building communities around these shared passions. Following your passions will not only develop your creativity and problem-solving abilities but could even open up professional doors.

So, let's embark on this voyage of self-discovery as we discover ways to broaden our interests, unearth new passions, and amplify life experiences.

Most common questions and answers about developing your interests

Q: How can I discover my passions?

A: Begin by trying new hobbies and discovering different activities. Pay attention to what brings you joy and fulfilment, taking note of any activities or subjects that seem particularly appealing or inspiring to you. Focus on discovering what motivates and energises you the most!

Q: What if I don't have any passions or interests?

A: Everyone has something they find enjoyable or intriguing that takes a little time and exploration to identify. Be open to trying different activities, and don't be intimidated to step outside your comfort zone when exploring your interests and passions.

Q: How can I find time to pursue my interests?

A: Make time by prioritising and incorporating your passions into your daily or weekly routine, perhaps altering it slightly or setting aside specific time blocks just for exploring them.

Q: How can I overcome self-doubt or fear of failure when exploring new interests?

A: Start small and focus on the process rather than its outcome. Give yourself permission to make mistakes and learn from them;

surround yourself with supportive people who will encourage and motivate you.

Q: How will pursuing my interests benefit me professionally?

A: Pursuing your passions can enhance creativity, problem-solving abilities, and overall job satisfaction while opening new doors in your industry or field.

Q: Can pursuing new interests improve my personal life?

A: Absolutely! Pursuing your passions can bring greater happiness and fulfilment into your life while creating opportunities for self-growth and discovery and developing meaningful relationships with like-minded individuals who share similar interests.

Myths and truths about developing your interests

Here are some myths and truths surrounding discovering your passions and enhancing your life:

Myth: To succeed in life and career success, one should only pursue interests that directly relate to those objectives.

Truth: Following your passions can bring both personal and professional growth. Engaging in activities that bring you pleasure can have an enormous impact on your overall well-being and happiness.

Myth: It's too late to pursue new interests.

Truth: Embark on a journey of self-discovery and allow yourself the freedom to experiment with new hobbies or interests at any stage in your life.

Myth: Pursuing one's interests is self-indulgent and a waste of time.

Truth: Dedicating time and energy to exploring your passions can provide numerous advantages, including enhanced creativity, improved mental health benefits, and personal fulfilment. Likewise, engaging with those of similar interests can open doors to networking with like-minded individuals as well as meaningful contributions made towards community betterment.

Myth: To pursue an interest, natural talent is necessary.

Truth: Talent may certainly help, but it's not required if you want to pursue your passions. Everyone starts somewhere, and mistakes and trial-and-error are OK as long as there is a growth mindset at play that encourages experimentation and learning as part of a path forward.

Myth: Pursuing one's interests requires extensive resources.

Truth: While some interests require more resources than others, there are numerous hobbies and activities you can enjoy on a budget or for free. Prioritise your interests carefully to allocate sufficient funds.

Explore your passions and understand why they make you interesting

Have you met anyone whose passion for their interests exuded charisma and energy? Discovering your own passions can make life more interesting for those around you while enriching your own life as well. Experiencing joy through following a passion can lead to personal fulfilment, enhanced creativity, problem-solving skills development, and even professional opportunities.

It's essential that when feeling stuck, one recognises that discovering their passions is a process of self-discovery. While it may take some time and experimentation before finding what truly motivates and excites you, once done, it will provide a sense of direction in life and a greater sense of purpose.

Participating in activities that bring you joy can have a positive effect on mental health and overall well-being and can help build new skills while creating connections between like-minded individuals.

If your interests have been neglected in your life, now is the time to prioritise them and devote some of your time each day to exploring them. Don't view pursuing your interests as selfish; consider them an investment in personal growth and happiness!

Here are five simple actions you can take to help discover the value of pursuing your interests and create a more fulfilling life:

Consider what you enjoyed as a child: Consider all the activities you enjoyed as a child before the pressures of adult life set in. Did you love drawing or playing an instrument, spending time outdoors, discovering new places, or simply exploring? Remembering these childhood interests will help you reacquaint yourself with them while sparking fresh ideas on how you can pursue them as an adult.

Attend events related to your interests: Explore local events, meetups, and workshops related to the things that interest you. Book clubs or photography courses can all provide great opportunities to explore your passions more deeply while meeting like-minded individuals.

Set small goals for yourself: Don't be overwhelmed by the daunting idea of exploring something new; set smaller, manageable goals instead. If painting is your interest, start small: paint for 30 minutes each day for one week as your initial goal, and gain confidence and momentum while doing so!

Venture outside your comfort zone: Experimentation can be terrifying but also exhilarating, so don't be intimidated by trying something totally foreign to your tastes; try something from a new cuisine, dance style, or hobby altogether and be open-minded; you may be amazed by what surprises are waiting. Embrace what seems foreign; you might just find your world is bigger than expected.

Share your passions: Don't be shy about expressing the interests that spark passions in others; you never know who may find inspiration in what you share. Sharing passions through social media or conversations with family and friends can create a sense of community around them and promote greater support for your passions.

Here are several things you could search on Google to discover new hobbies and passions:

Search "Hobby ideas for adults": This search query will bring up an abundance of resources that will help you discover hobbies that you may never have considered before.

Searching "How to discover your passions": This search will bring up articles and blogs offering advice on identifying and following up on passions that lie within yourself.

Searching "Classes near me": This search can help you locate classes or workshops focusing on various hobbies and interests in your local area, providing you with an opportunity to try something new in an organised and guided setting.

Establish a growth mindset that encourages exploration and learning

A growth mindset views challenges as opportunities for growth while understanding that failure is part of the learning process.

To foster a growth mindset, try shifting your perspective around failure. Instead of viewing it as an impending negative consequence, view failure as an opportunity for personal development and improvement. Celebrate successes, no matter how small, while acknowledging that growth requires patience and persistence.

Here are five items you could buy or search for online to foster a growth mindset that promotes exploration and learning:

Books on mindset: Consider purchasing Carol Dweck's "Mindset: The New Psychology of Success," as well as Annie Brock and

Heather Hundley's "The Growth Mindset Coach: A Teacher's Month-by-Month Handbook for Encouraging Students to Achieve."

Online courses: Search online courses related to developing a growth mindset, such as Coursera's "The Power of Mindset" course or Udemy's "Mindset Mastery".

Apps: Apps specifically tailored to cultivating a growth mindset exist, such as "Mindset: The Science of Success" or "Growth Mindset by Mindset Works". These apps offer daily reminders, exercises, and motivational quotes designed to shift your mindset.

Journals: If you want to develop a growth mindset, try purchasing journals such as "The 5-Minute Journal" or "The Growth Mindset Journal." These publications contain prompts and exercises designed to help you reflect on your mindset while encouraging a more positive, growth-driven perspective.

Workshops or classes: Take part in workshops or classes related to personal growth and development, such as meditation classes, yoga sessions, or personal development workshops. They can help foster an open mindset while opening up new possibilities.

Doing what interests you can be daunting, particularly if you fear what others might think. Yet developing the confidence to pursue those interests and share them with others is crucial for personal development and fulfilment.

One way to build confidence is by starting small. Practise your interests privately or with trusted friends before sharing them publicly. Remember that not everyone will share your interests; respect this fact when sharing them.

Here are 5 things you could post on social media to gain confidence in pursuing and sharing your interests:

- Share a post highlighting something new you have tried recently that you enjoyed, and encourage others to do the same!
- Post a picture of yourself doing something you love, along with an explanation as to why and its significance for you.
- Writing about something you've always been curious to try but haven't gotten around to is an effective way of gathering advice or insights from those with expertise in that area.
- Share an accomplishment related to your interests that helped increase your confidence in pursuing them.
- Engage your followers in conversation about their hobbies and passions, encouraging them to share what moves them.

5

Expanding Your Comfort Zone
HOW TO OVERCOME FEAR AND EMBRACE NEW EXPERIENCES

Are you tired of feeling stuck in your routine yet too afraid to explore new experiences? Have you ever found yourself contemplating taking that leap of faith to push beyond fear and explore what awaits beyond the walls of your current existence?

In this chapter, we'll examine the advantages of expanding your comfort zone and facing your fears to achieve personal development. We will address common questions and dispel myths associated with taking risks outside of one's comfort zone. We'll also examine practical strategies for overcoming fear and anxiety when trying new things, increasing self-awareness, and better recognising our individual limitations and strengths. Furthermore, we will consider how expanding our comfort zones can bring new experiences.

Risk-taking and facing fears can be terrifying, yet reaping great rewards can be equally as frightening. By building resilience and adaptability, we can gain greater faith in ourselves and trust our own judgement more readily. Additionally, by setting achievable goals that measure progress, we'll develop an eagerness for discovery, which can enrich all aspects of our lives.

Let's start, shall we?

Most common questions and answers about expanding your comfort zone

Q: Why should it be important to step outside your comfort zone?

A: Stepping outside your comfort zone can open the doors to personal growth and development as well as new experiences. Doing so also helps build resilience against uncertainties and change.

Q: How can I overcome fear and anxiety when starting new things?

A: Effective techniques for overcoming fear and anxiety include deep breathing, visualisation, positive self-talk, exposure therapy, and gradual exposure. Starting small will enable you to gradually build up to more challenging experiences.

Q: What can I do to expand my comfort zone and gain confidence?

A: Taking risks and facing your fears are two ways to do this. Trusting in yourself can increase self-assurance and trustworthiness. In addition, facing challenges head-on can build resilience while teaching valuable lessons from failure.

Q: How can I set achievable goals when expanding my comfort zone?

A: When setting goals, they must be specific, measurable, and attainable. Break larger objectives down into manageable steps for easier progression, and celebrate every achievement along the way!

Q: How can expanding my comfort zone lead to greater self-awareness?

A: By venturing outside your comfort zone and trying new activities, you may gain a deeper insight into yourself, discover hidden strengths and weaknesses, and gain an appreciation of both your limitations and potential.

Myths and truths regarding expanding your comfort zone

Myth: Sticking to what you know and avoiding taking risks is best.

Truth: Although staying within your comfort zone may feel safe and secure, staying there could also limit growth opportunities that could enable personal development and growth. Stepping outside your comfort zone and taking risks can open up new experiences that lead to growth opportunities and personal development.

Myth: Fear and anxiety are indicators that it may be time to abandon new experiences altogether.

Truth: While fear and anxiety may be natural responses to unfamiliar and uncertain circumstances, they don't indicate you should avoid them completely. By facing your fears head-on and managing anxiety effectively, you can expand your comfort zone while growing as an individual.

Myth: Expanding one's comfort zone is only necessary when working towards major life goals.

Truth: Broadening one's horizons should be practised in all aspects of life - big and small alike. Even small changes can contribute to personal development and help you feel more secure and fulfilled in everyday situations.

Myth: Fearlessness is required for expanding one's comfort zone.

Truth: Fear is an emotion everyone experiences; expanding one's comfort zone doesn't require having no fear at all; rather it means learning how to manage fear effectively so it doesn't hold them back from trying new experiences.

Myth: Stepping outside your comfort zone is always beneficial.

Truth: While expanding one's comfort zone can lead to personal growth and new opportunities, it may also be uncomfortable and challenging. It is essential to recognise all potential risks and difficulties as you prepare mentally and emotionally for them, though the rewards of going beyond one's comfort zone may far outweigh them!

Understanding the importance of risk-taking

Risk-taking is integral to human growth and development, whether quitting a job to start a business venture or moving to an unfamiliar city without knowing anyone there. Taking risks may seem terrifying at first, but they can bring many rewards, including increased self-confidence, greater self-awareness, and success in life.

Taking risks doesn't mean acting recklessly or without consideration; calculated risks involve carefully considering potential outcomes, weighing pros and cons, and making an informed decision based on available information. Many individuals have an aversion to risk, yet overcoming it may be key in terms of personal growth and development.

Here are three small things you could do today to embrace risk-taking:

- Select one area of your life where taking risks has become difficult for you; this could include your career, relationships, or hobbies. Consider one calculated risk you could take within this category, such as asking for a promotion or joining a new social group - and plan to implement this risk within one week.
- Beginning small is the key to building confidence. Taking an alternate route to work, tasting something unfamiliar for lunch, or taking up a new hobby can all help develop resilience against uncertainty and discomfort.
- Practise viewing challenges as opportunities for growth. Next time you face an obstacle, take some time to reflect on what lessons can be taken away from this experience and how it might strengthen your resilience over time.

Over time, this can help foster a more optimistic and growth-oriented perspective.

Why does embracing change help make me a people magnet?

While taking risks often has positive impacts on individual growth and achievement, it can also make you more attractive to others. People tend to admire those who show courage and confidence and are willing to step outside their comfort zones in pursuit of personal development and achievement.

By taking risks, you show others that you aren't afraid to face challenges and pursue your goals. This can be inspirational to those around you and may encourage them to take their own risks. Additionally, taking risks opens up opportunities to meet new people and expand your social circle.

Risk-taking also allows you to strengthen your credibility and reputation. When you take on challenging projects successfully, your accomplishments will become evident to others, which may open doors for new collaborations as people will want to work with someone with proven results who is also willing to take risks.

So if you want to become an attractive individual, embrace risk-taking. Take on new challenges with gusto and pursue your goals without fear. Not only will this allow for personal development and fulfilment, but it will also make you more appealing and open up new avenues of collaboration with others.

What are your gains from confronting your fears?

Fear can be an immense impediment, stopping people from following their dreams and reaching their goals. Overcoming fears can be liberating, leading to increased self-confidence and a sense of achievement. By confronting their fears head-on, individuals can gain a more comprehensive knowledge of themselves—both their limitations and strengths—while building greater self-awareness.

Fear can often be the gateway to greater success in life. Sometimes those things that cause us the most anxiety also present the greatest opportunities; for example, public speaking can open up an abundance of possibilities, from sharing ideas among colleagues to speaking at conferences.

Try these strategies to help you build up the confidence and courage to take risks:

- Write down all your fears, no matter how small.
- Select one small fear to face head-on and take one small action towards confronting it, such as making that phone call you have been putting off or trying a new food item.
- Utilise relaxation techniques such as deep breathing or meditation to reduce nerves and build resilience.
- Securing support from friends or therapists who can offer encouragement and accountability as you face your fears can also help immensely.
- Remind yourself of past victories and instances where you overcame fear by remembering past achievements, which will serve as reminders that you can do it again.

Understanding the importance of stepping outside your comfort zone and why it leads to personal development

Stepping outside one's comfort zone is essential for personal development and growth. Comfort zones represent what we know and feel secure with, and they can become our refuge when faced with unfamiliar experiences. By forcing ourselves out of this cocoon of familiarity and facing off against unknown challenges head-on, we open ourselves up to new experiences, developing both skills and abilities we may never have otherwise acquired.

Stepping outside one's comfort zone can be challenging, with fear, anxiety, and uncertainty all often serving as barriers to taking action. But it is essential to remember that expanding one's horizons requires gradual effort; setting small goals will enable individuals to build the skills and confidence required for facing new challenges head-on.

Try this:

Take an alternative route to work or school: Breaking away from your typical routine can be an effective way to add both novelty and discomfort to your life. By switching up the way you travel to and from work or school, taking a different path may help break you out of autopilot mode and keep you present in each moment of each day.

Try new cuisine: If you tend to stick with familiar foods, exploring unfamiliar cuisine can be an engaging and risk-free way to broaden your palette and cultural awareness. Be it Ethiopian, Korean, or Moroccan fare, trying something unfamiliar will broaden both your palate and your cultural knowledge!

Strike up a conversation with a stranger: While initiating conversations with strangers may be daunting, starting small by offering compliments or asking simple questions can help build confidence and social skills—and who knows, you might make new friends or learn something interesting along the way!

Discover effective methods for overcoming anxiety when engaging in new activities

Breaking through fear and anxiety is vital to leaving one's comfort zone and taking risks. There are various effective techniques available to individuals for managing fear and anxiety; one such technique is mindfulness meditation, which entails paying attention to the present moment without judgement or distraction. Through practising this form of awareness, one can learn to observe their thoughts and emotions without becoming overwhelmed by them.

Exposure therapy can also be an effective tool for managing fear and anxiety by gradually exposing oneself to what one fears, taking small, manageable steps before gradually building up to more challenging scenarios. Over time, exposure therapy helps desensitise individuals to their fears so that it becomes easier to face them in the future.

Try saying these to yourself:

- *"I know I am capable of meeting any challenge that may come my way."*
- *"I am courageous, trust my own decisions as the best decisions for me, and am open to new experiences and opportunities."*
- *"I am flexible and adaptable when faced with uncertainty and change.*
- *I deserve success and fulfilment."*
- *"I choose to focus on positive aspects instead of holding onto any negative ones, and I am committed to my personal development and growth."*

- *"I am proud of myself for taking risks and facing my fears head-on."*

Develop resilience and adaptability in the face of uncertainty and change

Resilience and adaptability are crucial skills for successfully navigating life's uncertainties. Everyday life presents its own set of unique challenges, so being able to adapt quickly to setbacks is vital for personal development and success. Building resilience requires adopting a growth mindset, which sees challenges as opportunities for personal development and learning.

One key way of building resilience and adaptability is by reframing challenges as opportunities. Instead of viewing setbacks as insurmountable barriers, you can view them as opportunities to learn and develop. By changing your perspective, you can gain more control over your life while strengthening your ability to cope with difficult circumstances.

Here are 5 additional things you can do to develop resilience and adaptability:

Purchase self-help books: There are numerous books on building resilience and adapting to change available, such as "The Resilience Factor" by Karen Reivich and Andrew Shatte or Rosamund Stone Zander and Benjamin Zander's "The Art of Possibility".

Use a journal: Writing down your thoughts and experiences can help give clarity and aid the processing of challenging emotions. Consider journaling daily or at times of high stress to boost resilience.

Invest in a life coach: Working with a life coach can provide personalised guidance and support in developing resilience and adaptability. When searching for the right professional to guide your development in certain areas, look for professionals with relevant expertise.

Attend a retreat or workshop: Retreats and workshops offer structured environments to develop resilience and adaptability. Look out for events focused on personal development or mindfulness, such as yoga retreats or meditation workshops, to find something relevant. Instead of dodging difficult situations, face them head-on and learn from them.

Practise gratitude: Focusing on the positive aspects of life and being grateful for what you have can help change your perspective and strengthen your ability to cope with stress and adversity.

Why doesn't everybody intentionally try to be resilient?

Many people have difficulty with intentionally testing themselves and pushing past their comfort zones to build resilience, due to the discomfort caused by facing our fears and taking risks.

Here are some reasons why it may be challenging for individuals to try things that will build their resilience:

Fear of failure: Many people fear failure and the emotions it brings with it, such as disappointment and shame, which can prevent them from taking risks and trying new activities that might help develop resilience and build strength. This fear prevents many people from taking chances that could help build their resilience.

Lack of self-confidence: Without self-confidence, people may struggle to trust in their abilities to overcome challenges and can feel powerless when facing challenging situations.

Resistance to change: Many individuals can be resistant to change and prefer what is comfortable over taking risks that could build resilience and create resilience in themselves. This may prevent them from taking the necessary steps needed for true personal development.

Overwhelm: Individuals may become overwhelmed by the demands of daily life and struggle to prioritise self-care and personal development.

Lack of support: People may lack access to resources or support networks needed for taking risks and building resilience.

Here are 20 easily implementable ideas to test your resilience today:

- Wake up an hour earlier than usual and use the extra time to do something productive or enjoyable.
- Take a cold shower to build mental and physical resilience.
- Practise deep breathing exercises to reduce stress and build emotional resilience.
- Take a different route to work or school to break your routine and build adaptability.
- Try a new type of cuisine or recipe to build openness to new experiences.
- Take a break from social media and digital devices to build focus and concentration.
- Have a conversation with someone you disagree with to build empathy and communication skills.
- Learn a new skill or hobby to build confidence and curiosity.
- Set a challenging fitness goal and work towards achieving it to build physical resilience.

- Write down three things you are grateful for each day to build gratitude and positivity.
- Meditate for a few minutes each day to build mindfulness and mental resilience.
- Take on a new responsibility or project at work or school to build resilience and perseverance.
- Volunteer for a cause you care about to build compassion and social resilience.
- Read a book or watch a movie that challenges your beliefs or worldview to build critical thinking skills.
- Spend time in nature to build a sense of peace and connection to the world around you.
- Practise saying no to requests or obligations that don't align with your values or goals to build assertiveness and self-care.
- Journal about your experiences and emotions to build self-awareness and reflection skills.
- Attend a social event or activity where you don't know anyone to build social resilience and connection.
- Face a fear or phobia in a safe and controlled environment to build courage and resilience.

Discover practical techniques for overcoming fear and anxiety when trying new things

If you find yourself anxious or fearful when facing unfamiliar experiences, there are practical techniques you can use to overcome such emotions.

Below are a few techniques you should try:

Practise mindfulness. Mindfulness is a technique in which you pay attention to the present moment without judgement. If you find yourself becoming anxious or fearful, take a few seconds to focus on breathing deeply and observe thoughts without passing judgement; this can help soothe and reduce anxiety levels in an instant.

Visualise Success: Visualising yourself successfully completing a new activity or task can boost confidence and reduce anxiety. Spend some time visualising the entire activity or task in detail, including how it will make you feel after it is done.

Break it down: If a new activity or task feels daunting, break it into smaller, manageable steps and focus on finishing each one before celebrating each small success.

Try this:

If the thought of going to the gym for an hour every day seems like too much work for you, break it into smaller, more manageable steps. For instance, committing just 10 minutes each day, such as going for a short walk or performing basic exercises such as squats and lunges, is easier for some than going straight for it all at once.

Once you've successfully accomplished 10 minutes of exercise each day for two weeks or more, rejoice and celebrate your achievement! Gradually increase the duration and intensity of your workouts until they add up to an hour-long session. Breaking it down into smaller pieces makes the task seem more manageable while building confidence and momentum for future tasks.

Don't hesitate to seek support from friends, family, or a professional when experiencing fear or anxiety. Sharing your worries can provide important perspectives as well as strategies for overcoming them.

Expanding your comfort zone requires moving into the unknown, which can involve facing uncertainty and change head-on. Building resilience and adaptability will enable you to tackle these challenges more successfully.

Here are a few methods of doing just that:

Positive thinking: Focusing on all that's good can help change the focus from uncertainty to what's going right in your life. Take some time each day to acknowledge all you are thankful for.

Some examples you could think about:

- *"Today, I am grateful for the warmth of the sun."*
- *"I appreciate my morning cup of coffee as well as the kindness shown me by my friends."*
- *"I am glad for this opportunity to learn something new today."*
- *"I am grateful for the soft bed I slept on last night."*
- *"I'm thankful for all of the laughter shared with my colleagues today."*

Recognise and accept failure: Failure is part of life and should be seen as an opportunity for learning and growth. When faced with failure, take time to analyse what you learned from it so you can apply this knowledge going forward.

Try thinking this instead:

- *"What did I learn from this experience?"*
- *"How can I use what I learned to improve next time?"*
- *"What can I do differently to avoid making the same mistake?"*
- *"What strengths and skills did I demonstrate in this situation?"*
- *"What can I do to support myself and cope with the disappointment?"*
- *"How can I reframe this failure as an opportunity for growth and development?"*

Stay curious

Indulge your sense of curiosity and wonder as you explore the world around you, opening yourself up to new experiences and perspectives while seeking opportunities for growth and learning.

How to get more curious:

Learn about new topics: Spend some time discovering topics that interest you by searching for articles, podcasts, and videos that delve deeper into subjects you find fascinating.

Try this:

You could try Googling some of the following:

- *"Top podcasts on [your favourite topic]"*
- *"Best YouTube channels for learning about [your area of interest]"*
- *"Interesting articles on [a specific topic you want to learn more about]"*
- *"Free online courses on [a subject you want to explore]"*
- *"Events or workshops on [a topic you're curious about] near me.*

Travel: Plan a journey to an unfamiliar locale, whether nearby or abroad. Get immersed in its culture while discovering its landmarks and history.

Try Googling these topics:

- *Best travel destinations for adventure seekers.*
- *Off-the-beaten-path travel destinations.*
- *Tips for solo travel.*
- *How to travel on a budget.*
- *Top travel experiences to have in [destination].*
- *Cultural events and festivals in [destination].*
- *Best restaurants and local cuisine in [destination].*

- *Travel safety tips and precautions.*
- *Sustainable travel options and ecotourism in [destination].*
- *Travel blogs and vlogs for inspiration and recommendations.*

Discover how expanding your comfort zone can lead to new opportunities and experiences

Stepping outside your comfort zone can bring new experiences you wouldn't otherwise encounter, opening up all kinds of exciting possibilities that you would not otherwise experience.

Exploring new things can help you develop new skills and expand your knowledge base, leading to a host of new opportunities both personally and professionally.

Try these:

Urban foraging: Discover edible plants hidden among city parks and green spaces.

Experimental cooking: Use unexpected ingredients to craft original dishes.

Cryptography: Master the art of creating and deciphering codes and cyphers.

Firewalking: Attend a workshop to gain courage and overcome your fear.

Animal tracking: Gain knowledge in animal tracking by learning signs and clues used by wildlife to navigate through their environment.

Calligraphy: Strengthen your artistic side while learning the art of beautiful writing.

Bonsai cultivation: Discover how to care for and cultivate miniature trees known as bonsai.

Historical Re-enactment Events (HREs): Gain knowledge about past events through participation while developing new skills through HRE events.

Metal detecting: Explore ways metal detectors can find hidden treasures.

Stepping outside your comfort zone can lead to personal growth and self-discovery. By facing fears and pushing past comfort zones, you may discover strengths and abilities you never knew were there.

Overcoming social anxiety

For some people, social anxiety can be a significant barrier to moving outside their comfort zone and experiencing new things. Social anxiety is a common condition characterised by fearful reactions in social situations or withdrawal from interaction altogether.

If you suffer from social anxiety, seeking professional assistance from a therapist or counsellor may help alleviate symptoms. A counsellor or therapist can offer guidance as you work to overcome fears and gain confidence enough to explore new experiences.

Cognitive-behavioural therapy (CBT) is an approach to psychotherapy that seeks to help individuals change negative thought patterns and behaviours that contribute to social anxiety. CBT seeks to teach individuals how to identify negative thoughts and beliefs, challenge them, and replace them with more constructive thoughts, as well as devise coping mechanisms to manage anxiety in social settings. CBT allows you to start practising by identifying any negative thoughts or beliefs you may hold about social situations and challenging them using evidence-based reasoning.

For instance, if you believe people will judge you negatively for making a silly remark in conversation, challenge this thought by reminding yourself that everyone makes mistakes and most people are generally understanding and forgiving of one another. With time and effort, you can replace negative beliefs with more optimistic thoughts to develop an empowered and confident mindset.

To find help with CBT for social anxiety, you could search "CBT for social anxiety", "CBT techniques for social anxiety", or "CBT therapy for social anxiety" on Google or YouTube. Alternatively, licensed therapists and counsellors who specialise in CBT for social anxiety in your local area or through online therapy services might also be beneficial.

As well as professional assistance, there are also several strategies you can employ to manage social anxiety. These may include practising relaxation techniques like deep breathing or meditation or gradually exposing yourself to social situations in a safe and supportive environment.

6

Building Confidence
HOW TO BOOST YOUR SELF-ASSURANCE AND BECOME MORE INTERESTING

Confidence is often seen as essential to reaching personal and professional success, yet many struggle to maintain it, leading them to experience feelings of inadequacy, anxiety, and missed opportunities. Building self-confidence takes effort, patience, and stepping outside one's comfort zone—an ongoing journey!

In this chapter, we will address some of the most frequently asked questions about confidence, including any myths that might be holding you back and their significance in building a strong sense of self-awareness. We will also discover practical techniques for increasing confidence and dispelling self-doubt.

By cultivating a positive mindset and clarifying your values, strengths, and goals, you can increase your sense of purpose and confidence. We'll explore the role self-esteem plays in becoming interesting to others as well as strategies for communicating more effectively and assertively.

With these tools and strategies, you can create an authentic yet compelling personal brand that not only boosts your confidence but also attracts and engages others.

So let's dive right in and begin building our confidence today.

Most common questions and answers about building confidence

Q: How can I become more self-confident?

A: There are various strategies available for increasing confidence, including self-care, reframing negative thoughts, setting achievable goals, and confronting fears through exposure therapy.

Q: Can being confident make me more appealing to others?

A: Yes, confidence can make you more engaged with those around you. Confident individuals tend to be seen as more attractive, charismatic, and inspiring, qualities that help foster strong relationships while simultaneously contributing to overall success in various aspects of life.

Q: How can I communicate more effectively and assertively?

A: Effective communication involves actively listening, expressing your ideas clearly, being confident while remaining assertive without being aggressive, using "I" statements when appropriate, avoiding interruption or judgement from others, and using eye contact while talking directly about yourself rather than interrupting or judging them as a way to engage in effective dialogue.

Q: What should I do if I experience rejection or failure?

A: Rejection and failure are inevitable parts of life; they should instead be seen as opportunities for personal growth and learning. When they occur, it's important to reflect on them as an experience to learn from. Take note of what was learned from it, and use this motivation as fuel to keep pushing to improve yourself further and take positive steps forward in your pursuits.

Q: How can I build resilience and bounce back from difficult situations?

A: Resilience can be increased through various techniques such as framing challenges as opportunities, practising self-care, seeking support from others, and focusing on personal development and learning. Adopt a growth mindset by viewing setbacks as opportunities rather than barriers that have to be surmounted to succeed in life.

Q: How can I build an authentic and compelling personal brand?

A: Establishing an engaging personal brand involves reflecting on your values, strengths, and goals before aligning actions and communications with these elements. Being honest about who you are while taking risks for growth is key.

Myths and truths about building confidence

Myth: Confidence is something you are born with; either you possess it or not.

Truth: Confidence is a skill that can be acquired over time through practice. It isn't something innately instilled within us; rather, it can be practised and improved upon over time with effort.

Myth: Confidence means always believing in oneself without ever doubting yourself.

Truth: Even those considered highly confident may experience times of self-doubt. Achieve true confidence by acknowledging and confronting fears and insecurities head-on.

Myth: Confidence lies solely in being outgoing and extroverted.

Truth: Confidence doesn't need to mean being loud and outgoing; it can come out quietly too. What matters is being comfortable with yourself and projecting self-assurance.

Myth: Confidence is only important in professional environments.

Truth: Confidence is crucial in all areas of life, from personal relationships to career success. When you feel secure within yourself, taking risks becomes easier and opportunities more abundant, ultimately leading to greater fulfilment in life.

Myth: Confidence is inborn and cannot be altered.

Truth: While certain individuals may naturally possess more self-assurance than others, any individual can increase their level of confidence through intentional effort and practice. By taking this path with an eye toward a growth mindset and perseverance, anyone can develop greater self-trust over time.

Confidence is an invaluable trait that can have a transformative effect on our personal and professional lives, from building strong relationships to attaining success and personal development.

While confidence may seem effortless to attain, building it may prove more of a challenge when faced with doubt, rejection, and failure. Developing self-assurance is vital, and there are practical techniques you can use to build it. We will go on to explore these next.

How to develop a strong sense of self and why it is necessary

A strong sense of self refers to having an accurate grasp of one's values, beliefs, and identity, which allows individuals to make decisions based solely on their thoughts and feelings rather than external factors influencing decisions made about them. Establishing such an identity helps build confidence.

Practise self-reflection to strengthen one's sense of self. This involves taking time to contemplate one's thoughts and emotions, identify areas of strength and weakness, and set goals aligned with one's values and beliefs. Through this process, individuals can gain clarity on their priorities, gain a sense of purpose, and build confidence in making decisions that represent who they truly are.

Try this:

Prepare a list: Make a list of values and beliefs that are significant to you. Don't worry about ranking them; just focus on what comes to mind.

Establish your values and beliefs: One effective strategy for developing a strong sense of self is to recognise one's values and beliefs. Values serve as guidelines that shape our behaviour and decision-making, while beliefs represent opinions or convictions that mould our worldview.

Here are some examples:

Honesty: You prioritise telling the truth even when it's difficult or uncomfortable.

Respect: You treat others with kindness and consideration, respecting their opinions and feelings, as well as acknowledging your responsibilities for their well-being.

Compassion: You strive to understand others while showing kindness and concern for their well-being.

Fairness: You believe in treating everyone fairly and justly.

Responsibility: You take ownership of your actions and their consequences.

Creativity: You enjoy expressing yourself creatively through art, music, writing, or other means.

Personal growth: Your focus is to constantly learn and advance yourself, as well as tackle new challenges head-on.

Environmentalism: You hold strong beliefs in protecting the natural world while making decisions that lessen its impact.

Spirituality: Your worldview embraces belief in a higher power or purpose and finds meaning by connecting to something outside yourself.

Say you're trying to decide whether or not to accept a job offer that would require relocation. In reflecting on your values and beliefs, ask yourself questions like, *"What am I prioritising in life?" "What are my long-term goals?"* Consider which is more important, stability or adventure. By considering all these aspects, you can make an informed decision that aligns with both your sense of self and your values.

Start living your life based on your values.

Evaluate past decisions: Reflect back on past decisions you have made and attempt to identify the values and beliefs that influenced those choices. Are they in line with what you truly value? If not, perhaps it is time for an evaluation to ensure they reflect who you really are as an individual.

Reflect on your upbringing: Consider how your upbringing and experiences may have shaped your values and beliefs, such as family, culture, or religion. Understanding this aspect can help provide greater clarity about your values and beliefs.

Consider your passions and interests: Passions and interests can provide insight into one's values and beliefs. For instance, being passionate about environmental issues could indicate an emphasis on sustainability or an interest in protecting the planet.

Understanding the importance of confidence for building relationships and achieving success

Confidence plays a crucial role in developing and maintaining relationships. People tend to gravitate toward those who exude confidence, as it suggests stability, self-assurance, and reliability—qualities that also translate well in professional settings where confidence leads to increased success and career advancement.

Building social confidence involves moving beyond one's comfort zone and taking risks, as well as prioritising authentic connections over trying to impress others. Through genuine connections, individuals can develop supportive networks of people that provide encouragement as they pursue personal and professional goals.

Here are a few actionable steps that can help build more self-assurance in any relationship or friendship:

Recognise and counter negative self-talk: When faced with social situations, identify any negative thoughts that arise about yourself and replace them with positive and self-affirming statements such as, *"I am worthy of their friendship"*. For instance, instead of thinking something like, *"I don't fit in here"*, make an affirming statement such as, *"I have a lot to give here."*

Active listening: Engage with others by attentively listening, asking follow-up questions, and showing empathy. This will build deeper connections while making others feel valued, all of which can build your confidence when faced with social situations.

Take initiative: Be bold in suggesting social activities or plans; this can demonstrate confidence and initiative while providing the chance to build stronger relationships. Remember to start small.

Establish boundaries: Setting boundaries is vitally important in any relationship or friendship, both personal and professional. Be clear in communicating your needs and expectations while remaining considerate of others' boundaries.

Focus on your strengths: Take notice of what makes you unique and utilise these characteristics and strengths when communicating with others to increase confidence and become more interesting. Doing this will lead to increased self-assurance as well as make interactions more engaging for them.

Be risky: Exercising initiative and taking risks can open up many new experiences. By pushing yourself to try new things and take on challenges, you'll increase your confidence and self-assurance.

Learn from your past experiences: Look back over past interactions and identify what worked and what didn't. Take this insight to adjust your approach and boost both social skills and confidence for future situations.

Practical techniques for conquering self-doubt

Building self-confidence involves altering both thought patterns and behaviours. One effective technique for developing it is self-affirmations, where positive statements are repeated back to oneself to bolster confidence and belief. Another approach involves challenging negative self-talk by recognising self-critical thoughts that arise and using affirming statements to counter them with positive affirmations.

Overcoming self-doubt requires taking action and facing fears head-on, including venturing out of one's comfort zone to try new things that may initially feel unfamiliar or frightening. This may take courage, but eventually taking risks and experiencing success can build confidence and help individuals overcome self-doubt.

Here are some suggestions as to how to overcome self-doubt:

Look for evidence: When feeling uncertain of yourself or doubting your abilities, look for evidence that contradicts negative thoughts. Make a list of accomplishments, skills, and positive feedback you've received from others, as this can help change your perspective and build confidence in your capabilities.

Outwork self-doubt: Push yourself out of your comfort zone by challenging yourself to take steps that feel uncomfortable or scary - even if they may seem terrifying at the time! As you take action and face down your fears, your confidence will increase over time. Set small goals along the way, and celebrate each small success to keep yourself motivated.

Do it over and over: Repetition is key when it comes to overcoming self-doubt. Start facing your fears head-on until you start feeling more at ease with yourself and confident in your abilities. For instance, if public speaking makes you nervous, start off speaking before smaller audiences before gradually increasing to larger ones.

Discovering how confidence can increase interest and engagement

Confidence can help individuals appear more intriguing and engaging to others by signalling authenticity and conviction. People are drawn to those who exhibit confidence in their beliefs, and abilities, willingness to take risks, and willingness to be themselves; being interesting requires remaining true to oneself while offering unique perspectives as well as being open to learning and growth.

Try this:

Here are some questions you could ask to show confidence in a conversation:

- *"Can you tell me more about your perspective on that?"*
- *"How do you think we could approach this problem differently?"*
- *"I have a different opinion on this matter; would you like to hear it?"*
- *"What are your thoughts on [a specific topic]?"*
- *"I'm interested in learning more about [a specific area]. Do you have any recommendations or resources?"*

How to become assertive

Assertive communication can also help build self-confidence, as this method involves being direct and clear while still acknowledging and respecting others' opinions and feelings. People with low self-esteem may struggle with being assertive, either by being too passive and avoiding conflict or by becoming aggressive or disrespectful in their approach to others.

To become more assertive, begin by recognising and practising assertive communication techniques such as using *"I"* statements to express thoughts and emotions, maintaining eye contact, and using an assertive tone of voice. Remember to also listen actively while showing respect for others' opinions.

Here are some examples of assertive communication statements:

- *"I find it frustrating when you don't live up to your commitments. Can we talk about ways we can avoid this happening again in the future?"*
- *"Thanks for listening, but my opinion remains unchanged on this matter."*
- *"I need some time to think over this before making my decision. Can we discuss it later?"*
- *"I understand your viewpoint, but to take care of myself, I must set boundaries."*
- *"I appreciate our relationship, but I don't agree with how you are treating me. Can we come together and find a solution together?"*

Your personal brand

Building an impressive personal brand is another essential step toward increasing self-confidence. A personal brand encompasses the unique combination of skills, experiences, and values that you bring to the table.

By clearly communicating this brand to potential employers and collaborators alike, it will help establish you as an authority within your field while simultaneously attracting opportunities that align with your values and goals.

To create an engaging personal brand, the first step should be identifying your strengths, values, and passions.

Consider how these assets could be combined to form a unique value proposition that sets you apart from others. Once identified, build your professional online presence through LinkedIn profiles or personal websites while consistently communicating your brand through communication and behaviour.

So, how can you build a strong personal brand? Here are a few ways you can do this:

Optimise your profile: After choosing the appropriate platform, ensure your profile is complete and showcases your skills, experiences, and accomplishments engagingly. Use keywords specific to your industry so they will appear when someone searches for your name.

Sharing thought leadership content: Sharing articles, blogs, and other relevant pieces can establish you as an authority in your field while increasing visibility and creating new connections.

Showcase your work: If you have examples of your work, such as portfolio pieces or completed projects, consider including them on your profile or website to provide potential employers and clients with a better idea of your skills and capabilities. This may help them understand more quickly the value you bring them.

Engage with your network: Engaging with your network is an integral component of building an online presence. Engage with them by commenting on their posts, sharing their content, and reaching out to new people in your industry.

Be consistent: Maintaining an effective online presence requires consistency. Update your profile or website frequently, share new content, and engage with your network to remain visible and relevant in your industry.

Self-esteem is also an essential ingredient in becoming an engaging person. Achieving this means taking risks, following your passions, and sharing unique perspectives—qualities that make you more attractive and fascinating to those around you.

To boost your self-esteem, focus on developing a positive image of yourself and engaging in activities that bring joy and satisfaction.

Surround yourself with supportive individuals who acknowledge who you are as a unique individual. Keep in mind that self-esteem isn't fixed; it can be increased with consistent effort.

In summary, developing self-confidence is integral to personal and professional success as well as fulfilling relationships. By understanding its importance, learning practical techniques for building it, and taking proactive steps toward cultivating a positive mindset and personal brand, you can become more engaging and assured in all areas of life.

7

Enhancing Your Social Skills
HOW TO CONNECT WITH OTHERS
AND BUILD MEANINGFUL
RELATIONSHIPS

Are you feeling intimidated in social situations and finding it hard to connect with people? If that sounds familiar, this chapter could be exactly what you've been looking for!

By reading this chapter, you will not only gain practical strategies for improving communication, active listening, empathy, and relationship-building but also the self-assurance to navigate social situations more confidently and build meaningful relationships.

Learning how to build rapport and create an ideal first impression is just the start; we will also cover how to handle difficult conversations and conflict resolution. Furthermore, effective networking strategies, cultural differences, and effectively communicating with individuals from diverse backgrounds are covered as well.

Let's get started by answering two of the most common questions asked about social skills, followed by some myths and truths.

The two most commonly asked questions about social skills

Q: Why are social skills necessary?

A: Social skills are indispensable in cultivating meaningful relationships. They enable us to communicate effectively, establish rapport, and address conflicts positively. Good social skills also play a pivotal role in professional success, as they enable us to network effectively with colleagues and advance our careers.

Q: Can social skills be learned?

A: Yes, social skills can be learned and improved upon through practice. While some individuals may naturally possess greater social graces than others, every individual can benefit from honing their interpersonal abilities by practising effective communication, active listening, and empathy—building deeper connections with people while creating meaningful relationships.

Myths and truths about social skills

Myth: Social skills are only important for extroverted people.

Truth: Social skills are important for everyone, regardless of their personality type. Introverted people can benefit from improving their social skills just as much as extroverted people.

Myth: Social skills are innate and cannot be learned.

Truth: While some people may have a natural aptitude for social skills, they can be learned and improved upon with practice and effort.

Myth: Social skills are only necessary for professional success, not personal relationships.

Truth: Social skills are important for both personal and professional success. They help us connect with others, build trust, and positively resolve conflicts.

Myth: People are either born with good social skills or they're not.

Truth: Social skills can be learned and developed over time. While some people may have a natural talent for socialising, everyone can benefit from practising and improving their social skills.

Myth: Social skills are just about being polite and friendly.

Truth: While being polite and friendly is important, social skills encompass much more than that. They also include effective communication, active listening, empathy, conflict resolution, networking, and cultural awareness.

By dispelling these common myths and embracing the truths about social skills, we can all work towards becoming more socially skilled and building more meaningful relationships in our personal and professional lives.

Communication is at the core of developing social skills. Improving one's communication abilities is integral to developing and maintaining relationships, as effective dialogue should be clear, concise, and respectful.

Personal relationships also rely heavily on social skills for success; these enable us to connect with others, build trust, and form meaningful bonds. These tools also enable us to communicate efficiently, amicably resolve conflicts, and empathise with those we interact with.

Here are some tips for strengthening your communication abilities using social skills:

Speak clearly and confidently: To effectively communicate your message, employ a confident tone of voice when speaking your thoughts aloud.

Here's an example of how speaking clearly and confidently can make a difference:

Scenario 1: You are in a job interview. Your interviewer asks you to describe your qualifications and experience. You respond by speaking timidly, stumbling over words, and failing to provide clear examples of your achievements.

Scenario 2: You are in a job interview. Your interviewer asks you to describe your qualifications and experience. You respond in an authoritative and confident voice, offering clear examples that highlight your qualifications, experience, and strengths.

In the second scenario, your clear and confident communication style leaves an excellent first impression with interviewers, increasing the odds that they offer you the job. Being clear and confident helps effectively convey your message while projecting confidence and competence to others.

Listen actively: Listening is an integral component of communication, so practise active listening by giving the speaker your full attention, asking any necessary questions, and clarifying any misunderstandings as soon as they arise.

Here are some examples of questions you can ask to practise active listening:

- *"Can you tell me more about that?"*
- *"How did that make you feel?"*
- *"What do you mean by [specific term or phrase]?"*
- *"Could you clarify what you said about [specific point]?"*
- *"What was your thought process behind [specific decision or action]?"*
- *"How would you like to proceed from here?"*
- *"What are your goals in this situation?"*
- *"Can you give me an example of [specific point]?"*
- *"What do you hope to achieve by [specific action or decision]?"*
- *"Is there anything else you'd like to share with me about this topic?"*

By actively listening and asking questions, you can better understand the speaker's perspective and clarify any misunderstandings, leading to more effective communication and a stronger relationship.

By being more interested in them, you will be seen as a more interesting conversationalist!

Be concise: Avoid using complex language or unnecessary words, and focus on getting your message across clearly and quickly.

Empathy: This is the ability to understand and share another person's feelings. It is an invaluable social skill, allowing us to form deeper connections with those around us.

Here are some strategies for strengthening empathy:

Put yourself in their place: An effective way of understanding another's perspective and responding appropriately is by trying to envision their feelings and thoughts as you attempt to put yourself in their position. This allows you to make an accurate judgement based on their input.

Be kind: Show genuine concern and support for another to build trust and strengthen the relationship. This can help create positive experiences between individuals.

Building rapport and making an impressive first impression

Rapport is the sense of trust and understanding between two individuals that develops over time. Rapport building is an essential social skill that can help us form meaningful relationships.

Here are some strategies for developing rapport:

Explore common interests or values: By exploring commonalities between both parties, it may help establish deeper ties and allow for stronger interpersonal interactions.

Here are a few approaches for discovering shared interests or values:

Ask open-ended questions: Use open-ended queries that allow the other person to elaborate on their interests or values, such as, *"What hobbies do you enjoy doing?"* or *"Which values are most significant to you?"*

Share your interests or values: Express your own interests or values and try to determine if there are any similarities with those of another individual. For instance, *"I love hiking; do you take part in any outdoor activities?"* or *"I place great importance on honesty and integrity - do you share these qualities too?"*

Create common interests: In group settings, attempt to find something that unites all parties involved. For example, if everyone loves a certain genre of music or cuisine, an outing or event centred around this could be planned around that shared interest.

Join a club or group: Consider joining a club or group that shares your interests or values; this can create opportunities to meet others with similar perspectives.

Show genuine interest: Be sincere in expressing genuine curiosity about another by asking thoughtful questions and actively listening to their responses.

Here are a few ways you can demonstrate genuine interest:

Ask thoughtful questions: Ask thoughtful questions that demonstrate you are interested in understanding more about someone. For example, *"Why did you decide to pursue that career or hobby?"* or *"How has that inspired you?"*

Respond with follow-up questions: Build upon what the other person has told you by asking follow-up questions that demonstrate you are actively listening and seeking more knowledge. For instance, *"That was really interesting; what have been some of the challenges associated with your hobby?"*

Showing genuine interest can make you an engaging conversationalist because it shows that you respect their opinions and ideas. Furthermore, by asking thoughtful questions and listening carefully to their answers, you can forge stronger interpersonal bonds and form deeper, more meaningful relationships.

Be authentic: Stay true to yourself and avoid trying to become someone you aren't. Being authentic helps build trust and respect among peers and stakeholders alike.

Fostering confidence and self-assurance to navigate social situations with ease

Confidence and self-assurance are keys to effectively navigating social situations with ease. They enable us to communicate more efficiently, build trust among peers, and address conflicts more positively.

Here are some strategies for building confidence and self-assurance:

Practice: Rehearsing social skills in low-stress situations, such as with friends or family, can help build confidence and increase self-assurance.

Here are some ways you can do this:

Small talk: Develop skills in initiating and maintaining conversational exchanges with friends or family members by asking open-ended questions and sharing personal stories about yourself.

Bring up engaging news or facts: Share an interesting news story or fact you discovered that could spark an engaging dialogue.

Discuss your hobbies or passions: Sharing your hobbies or passions with others and learning about theirs will allow you to find common ground and build lasting connections.

Discussion about travel experiences: Sharing or gathering others' travel tales, can lead to stimulating dialogue about diverse cultures and experiences.

Share a personal accomplishment: Share any recent accomplishment, such as finishing a project or reaching a goal, with others and ask them about theirs.

Discuss current events: Engaging and thought-provoking discussions could ensue by exploring current or recent happenings that generate stimulating conversations.

Be assertive: Express your opinions and needs clearly while remaining considerate of others' perspectives.

Practise nonverbal communication: Exercising proper body language - such as making eye contact and smiling while speaking in an approachable tone of voice, will aid your communication efforts significantly.

Prepare: If you know you will encounter a social situation that causes anxiety, prepare beforehand by practising what to say or do and visualising a successful outcome.

Focus on strengths: Recognising and appreciating your strengths can help build confidence and self-assurance, leading to improved outcomes in terms of confidence and self-assurance.

Handling difficult conversations and conflict resolution

Conflict and difficult conversations are inevitable in social situations; being able to handle them efficiently is an invaluable social skill.

Here are a few strategies for handling difficult conversations and conflict resolution:

Maintain calm: When faced with difficult conversations or conflicts, remaining calm and composed is of the utmost importance. Take deep breaths if needed, or count to 10 to remain relaxed.

Listen actively: Active listening is essential in all communication. Listening closely and understanding someone else's perspective are key components of effective dialogue.

Focus on the problem: Instead of attacking an individual directly, turn your attention towards solving the issue at hand together with them. Find a mutually acceptable solution that meets everyone's needs.

Here are a few phrases you could use to focus on the issue and come up with mutually acceptable solutions:

- *"Let's work together to find a solution that meets the needs of both parties involved."*
- *"I understand your position; let's see if there's an approach that meets both our requirements."*
- *"Can we brainstorm some possible approaches together until we arrive at something acceptable?"*
- *"My goal is to find an amicable resolution that addresses this issue without making anyone uncomfortable. Let's approach this situation with an open mind and see what solutions we can come up with together."*
- *"It is of utmost importance to me that we find a solution that considers everyone's needs and interests. Can we work towards that together?"*

Discovering how to network effectively and establish long-lasting relationships

Networking is building relationships with others to achieve personal or professional goals. It's an integral component of social skills that can help us advance in our careers or meet personal objectives.

Here are some tips on effective networking:

Attend events: Networking events, conferences, and workshops related to your field can be great opportunities to meet new people and expand your network.

Follow up: After meeting someone new, be sure to follow up. This can help build the relationship and ensure you remain top of mind with them.

Here are a few phrases you could use when following up with someone:

- "I had such a wonderful time meeting you earlier today! I wanted to see if we had any time for coffee and conversation later?"
- "I just wanted to extend my gratitude for taking the time and meeting with me last week. Our conversation was really informative."
- "I've been reflecting on our discussion since then and would like to see if any additional insights or thoughts have surfaced since our initial dialogue."
- "I had the pleasure of meeting you at [event] and wanted to see if there was any interest in collaborating on a project together."

By using these phrases, you can follow up with someone you've met and strengthen the relationship. It will also potentially open doors for collaboration or networking opportunities in the future.

Always ensure your follow-up messages are courteous, respectful, and genuine!

Provide value: Giving something of worth to others—such as knowledge, skills, or resources—can help build trust and respect between us all.

Enhancing emotional intelligence and self-awareness

Emotional intelligence refers to our ability to understand and regulate both our own emotions as well as those of others with greater self-awareness.

Emotional intelligence is an essential social skill that helps build stronger relationships as well as personal and professional success.

Here are some tips for developing emotional intelligence:

Practise self-reflection: Set aside some time each day for reflection on your emotions and reactions in various situations. This will enable you to gain a better understanding of yourself as an individual as well as how you affect interactions with others.

Here are some questions you could ask yourself during self-reflection:

- *"What emotions did I experience in a particular situation?"*
- *"How did I react to those emotions, and why?"*
- *"Did my reactions have a positive or negative impact on my relationships with others?"*
- *"How can I better manage my emotions in future situations?"*
- *"What are my values, and how do they guide my actions and interactions with others?"*
- *"What are my strengths and weaknesses in social situations?"*

- *"How do my past experiences shape my current behaviour and interactions with others?"*
- *"What are some of my personal biases, and how do they impact my interactions with people from different backgrounds or with different perspectives?"*
- *"How can I improve my communication and active listening skills?*
- *What steps can I take to develop my emotional intelligence and self-awareness?"*

Learn to control emotions effectively: Tactics to effectively manage emotions include deep breathing or taking breaks when needed; doing this can help you prevent responding impulsively in social settings.

Take a breather when emotions overwhelm you to gain control and prevent reactive responses in social situations.

By giving yourself time to collect your thoughts before reacting emotionally, taking a step back allows you to respond more thoughtfully and effectively and build stronger interpersonal relationships based on respectful dialogue.

In addition, by learning to control emotions effectively, you may reduce stress and anxiety in social encounters, leading to a more enjoyable social experience overall.

Gaining an understanding of cultural differences and communicating effectively with people of diverse backgrounds

As our world grows increasingly diverse, understanding cultural differences and communicating effectively across borders are becoming ever more crucial.

Here are some tips for gaining insight into and communicating effectively across cultures:

Educate yourself: Learning more about different cultures can help you understand and communicate with people from diverse backgrounds more easily.

Here are a few steps you can take to educate yourself about different cultures:

Study books or articles: Reading books or articles about different cultures will give you an in-depth knowledge of their customs, beliefs, and values.

Attend cultural events: Attending cultural events such as festivals or celebrations in your local area allows you to immerse yourself in various cultures while learning more about them.

Staying in the know: Watch documentaries or films about different cultures to gain a deeper insight into their history, traditions, and daily lives.

Discover a new language: Learning a foreign language can help you communicate more efficiently with people from various cultures and gain greater insights into their perspectives.

Engage with people from different cultures: Make an effort to engage with individuals from various cultural backgrounds and engage in discussions to gain more insights into their experiences and perspectives.

Take courses or workshops: For an enhanced education on different cultures, enrolling in courses or workshops focused on diversity, cultural competency, or intercultural communication is an effective way to deepen knowledge.

Be respectful: Show respect for other cultures and traditions by refraining from making assumptions or stereotyping based on cultural differences.

Active listening: When communicating with people from various backgrounds, active listening can be particularly useful in understanding each perspective and clearing up any misunderstandings that may exist. Listen carefully and ask any necessary questions to best represent their opinions and clarify any ambiguities.

Overall, by being more assured in your social skills, you will make all the conversations you have more interesting, and increasing self-assurance will enable more meaningful encounters between yourself and others.

8

Travelling And Cultivating Experiences
HOW TO BROADEN YOUR HORIZONS AND DEVELOP AN INTERESTING LIFE

Do you ever wonder why some people seem to have so many captivating tales to tell? Typically, this is because they've experienced multiple cultures first-hand, giving them a unique viewpoint and amassing amazing experiences to share with others.

In this chapter, we'll explore how travel can enhance and enrich your life. I will dispel common myths and fears surrounding travel and provide practical techniques for planning and budgeting trips abroad, as well as offer tips for making the most of experiences by immersing yourself in local cultures.

But even if travel is out of the question right now, don't despair; I have you covered! I will teach you how to create experiences in your daily life and communicate them effectively to make you even more interesting!

By reading this chapter, not only will you discover the advantages of travel for personal growth and development but you'll also gain insight into how travel can enhance communication skills while creating an expansive network of people who share your enthusiasm for adventure and exploration.

Most common questions and answers about travel

Q: Why is travel important?

A: Travel allows you to expand your horizons and experience other cultures first-hand, giving you new perspectives, insights, experiences, and ultimately personal growth and development.

Q: How can I afford travel?

A: You can budget for travel by creating a travel fund, planning ahead and selecting cost-effective options such as low-cost flights or budget accommodations.

Q. If I can't afford travel, what options do I have?

A: Even without travelling you can still create memories in everyday life by exploring your local area, trying new activities, and learning new skills. Furthermore, online communities allow travellers to share experiences and travel tips.

Q: How can I maximise my travel experience?

A: You can make the most out of your travel experiences by immersing yourself in local culture, sampling cuisine native to that destination, and engaging in activities unique to that area. Connecting with locals or fellow travellers may offer additional insights or recommendations for future destinations.

Q: How can travel make me more interesting?

A: Travel can give you access to a wealth of unique experiences and stories to share, providing an added dimension of interest that makes you an all-around more engaging person. Furthermore, travelling can enhance communication skills as you connect with people from various backgrounds.

Q: How can I overcome my fear of travelling?

A: Start small by planning a short trip with friends or family nearby, researching the destination in advance to reduce anxiety and planning ahead to maximise enjoyment and personal growth through travel.

Q: How can I make my travel experiences more sustainable?

A: To enhance sustainability on your trips, choose eco-friendly accommodations, reduce waste production and support local businesses while selecting sustainable transportation options such as walking, bicycling or public transit.

Q. How can I create new experiences even when not travelling?

A: Incorporating new experiences into daily life means trying out different activities, learning new skills, and engaging with your local community. Explore nearby destinations or plan a weekend getaway to break up the routine and give your mind something different to focus on!

Q: How can I communicate my travel experiences effectively to others?

A: To effectively share your travel experiences with others, focus on sharing details and insights about the destination and culture that are specific and engaging for that audience. Alternatively, storytelling techniques like creating narrative arcs or emphasising sensory details may make these stories even more captivating for your listeners.

Myths and truths about travelling

Myth: Travel is expensive and only for the wealthy.

Truth: While some forms of travel may be expensive, there are affordable options such as low-cost flights, budget accommodations and public transport that make travel accessible for everyone. Furthermore, budgeting travel requires setting aside funds or planning trips during off-peak seasons for greater savings.

Myth: Travel can be dangerous.

Truth: While travel does pose risks, there are steps travellers can take to minimise them - like researching their destination in advance, taking necessary precautions, and being aware of their surroundings. Many destinations also boast robust tourism industries which make travelling safe.

Myth: Travel is a waste of both time and money.

Truth: Travelling can be an invaluable investment in personal growth and development, offering new experiences, perspectives, cultural awareness and the chance to escape daily stresses. Additionally, travelling can boost creativity, improve communication skills and offer respite from stressors such as work.

Myth: Experienced travellers must enjoy travel.

Truth: Anyone, no matter their level of experience, can appreciate travel. Being new can even be beneficial as it allows one to approach each new place with curiosity and wonder. Furthermore, many resources exist specifically for new travellers such as blogs, guidebooks and travel communities that provide helpful support.

Fears around doing this before and how to overcome them

Fear of the unknown: Many are nervous to step outside their comfort zones and explore what lies beyond. However, travelling is all about experiencing new things! To combat your fears about travel and explore unknown territories safely, begin researching your destination, creating a plan and setting realistic expectations - then connect with other travellers or locals for advice or insight!

Fear of safety: Safety concerns when travelling are legitimate, but shouldn't be an excuse not to explore new experiences. To overcome them, research your destination beforehand, stay aware of your surroundings, and take necessary precautions such as keeping valuables secure, avoiding unsafe areas and purchasing travel insurance to provide peace of mind.

Fear of budgeting: Travel can be expensive, making budgeting intimidating for some travellers. To overcome this fear, start by setting realistic budgets, researching affordable travel options and using budgeting apps or tools to track expenses.

Tips on how to overcome budgeting fears:

Create realistic budgets: Before planning your trip, establish realistic budgets. Think through expenses such as accommodation, transportation, food and activities before setting a daily or weekly budget based on the total expense of travel.

Example: If your budget for travelling to Europe for two weeks is $2,000 ($143 a day), set an expenditure budget that encompasses accommodation, food, transportation and activities expenses.

Research affordable travel options: Research your affordable travel options such as budget airlines, hostels or public transportation to find an option that meets your travel budget. Don't forget about deals or discounts for activities or tours as another way of saving money!

Example: Instead of opting for an expensive hotel room, consider staying at a hostel or renting one on Airbnb. Take advantage of free walking tours or look for affordable activities such as visiting local parks or museums.

Fear of loneliness: Travelling alone may seem intimidating at first, and fearing being alone is enough to deter many from exploring travel experiences. Yet solo travel can also be extremely rewarding and offer an opportunity for self-discovery. To combat loneliness during solo travel experiences, joining a group tour or connecting with fellow travellers through online communities or social media could help ease some anxiety; engaging locals by visiting them and learning their culture may also provide assistance.

The benefits of travel for you and your self-esteem

Travel can help build confidence: Experiences abroad can give you a newfound sense of assurance in yourself and your abilities, giving you more reasons to share stories about overcoming challenges and venturing beyond your comfort zone. This may make travelling even more fascinating!

Travelling alone or with a small group can help foster independence and build self-reliance, providing opportunities to explore destinations on your terms while sharing tales about solo journeys with other travellers.

Improved communication skills: Travelling to countries whose language and customs differ significantly from your own can help develop communication and cultural sensitivity, making you more interesting by connecting with locals and sharing insights into different ways of life.

Exposure to new perspectives: Travel can open you up to new viewpoints, expanding your worldview and giving you a more nuanced understanding of issues and topics. It can make you a more interesting travel companion as you gain exposure to diverse viewpoints that expand the way you perceive things and make decisions.

Greater creativity: Exploring different sights, sounds, and cultures can spur creativity and spark innovative new ideas that may make you more interesting by providing unique perspectives on various subjects. This can make life more exciting!

Think of it like this…

Travel opens your mind to new ideas and perspectives, such as cultures, customs, and traditions you may never have encountered otherwise. Travel can widen horizons while challenging assumptions, leading to greater creativity and innovation.

Example: While travelling in Japan, a graphic designer might find inspiration from traditional Japanese design, its clean and minimalist aesthetic, and then go on to develop their own signature style that incorporates these elements.

Travel is an invaluable opportunity to develop problem-solving skills and creativity, offering travellers ample chances to adapt quickly to unfamiliar terrain and overcome unexpected challenges.

Example: Travelers often encounter unexpected transportation delays and must devise innovative solutions to reach their destination, which requires problem-solving skills that go beyond conventional thinking.

Breaking routines: Travel can break you out of your routine and open your mind up to new experiences, stimulating creativity and leading to innovative thinking.

Example: Travel can help a writer overcome writer's block and inspire them to create something fresh and new in their stories.

Experience different art and culture: Travel provides the opportunity to encounter various forms of art, music, and culture that can spark creativity and bring fresh perspectives into one's own artwork.

For instance, an artist might take inspiration from vibrant street art in a foreign city to incorporate into their own creation.

Understand the importance of travel and new experiences in personal growth and development

Travelling and experiencing other cultures is more than just an exciting adventure; they provide an opportunity for personal growth and development.

By breaking out of your comfort zone and immersing yourself in new experiences, travelling can offer new perspectives, help build self-awareness, and improve overall well-being - studies have even demonstrated this fact! Interestingly enough, studies have also proven travel's positive benefits such as increasing creativity, decreasing stress levels, and promoting overall well-being.

Travel can make you more interesting by giving you an entirely unique view of the world. Learning about different cultures and lifestyles will broaden your perspective, increase empathy and understanding and make you more relatable to others.

Furthermore, sharing travel stories with others makes for engaging conversation starters! To keep the discussion dynamic and inclusive, try engaging the other person by including them in your dialogue.

Here are some helpful tips on how you can do just that:

Ask about their travel experiences: To make the person you are speaking to feel engaged with what is being discussed, ask about any interesting travel stories they might have had themselves. This can facilitate more interactive discussions.

Example: *"Have you ever been to Thailand? I discovered an odd fruit there and would love for you to experience it too!"*

Ask for their recommendations: Show that you are interested in them by seeking recommendations of travel destinations or activities you would like to try. Ask for their opinions about these activities. This shows your interest and fosters more collaborative discussions between both of you.

Example: *"I'm planning a trip to Canada soon. Have you been? Can you recommend any must-see sights or activities?"*

Relate your travel experiences to theirs: When conversing, attempt to relate your travel experiences directly to their interests to create more engaging conversations that resonate with both parties involved. Doing this can make any conversation feel more personalised and relevant to one or both individuals involved in it.

Example: *"You mentioned you enjoy hiking. Have you been to Machu Picchu yet? It is an incredible hiking destination filled with so much history to discover!"*

Engaging the other person and drawing out their interests and experiences can make the discussion more interesting and inclusive, creating a dialogue that deepens relationships and bonds with those you encounter.

Here are a few specific ideas and examples for setting travel goals or creating a vision board to maximise your travel experience:

Create a bucket list: Setting aside time each month or quarter for creating your bucket list can provide motivation to plan trips and get the most out of your experience.

Example: *"My bucket list entails visiting all seven continents, diving the Great Barrier Reef and witnessing the Northern Lights in Iceland."*

Establish travel goals: For each trip you take, set specific travel goals such as learning a new language or food item or experiencing new cultures and customs. Doing this can motivate you to step outside your comfort zone.

Example: *"My goal for my trip to Italy is to learn the art of homemade pasta making and try at least one new Italian dish daily."*

Craft a vision board: Use images, quotes and other visual aids to craft a collage that represents your travel goals and aspirations. Create something inspiring and motivational!

Example: *My vision board includes pictures of the Eiffel Tower and Great Wall of China as well as a quote that states, 'Travel is the only purchase that makes us richer.'*

Establishing travel goals or creating a vision board can help motivate and inspire you to make the most of your travel experiences.

Setting travel goals provides clear direction and purpose to your trips, which makes them even more satisfying and unforgettable.

Once your destination selections have been selected, research alternative forms of travel such as volunteering or joining cultural exchange programs for added enrichment.

Make time to reflect upon and document your experiences by journaling or blogging them so you can internalise and share them with others.

Practical techniques for travel planning and budgeting

Online searches: To learn practical techniques for planning and budgeting for travel, you may want to try searching for the following keywords on Google:

- "Budget travel tips"
- "How to plan a trip on a budget"
- "Cheap travel ideas"
- "Cost-effective travel options"
- "Travel budget calculator"

When it comes to considering alternative modes of transportation, you could try searching for specific transportation options such as:

- "Train travel for budget travellers"
- "Budget bus travel options"
- "Tips for budget road trips"
- "Affordable bike rental options for travellers"

Using these keywords can help you find useful resources and information on how to plan and budget for your travel. It can also help you find alternative transportation options that may be more cost effective and offer a unique travel experience.

Search for free activities: Many destinations provide free activities such as museums, parks or cultural events; researching these options before travelling can save money while still giving you an enjoyable experience.

Opt for local transport: Utilising public transit such as buses, trains or subways can be more cost-effective and allows you to experience local culture first-hand while connecting with local people.

Consider travel during off-peak seasons: Travelling during off-peak seasons can often result in lower travel and accommodation costs as well as the chance to avoid crowds and have a more authentic experience.

Utilise budgeting apps or tools: There are various budgeting apps and tools available that can assist in keeping tabs on travel expenses, creating an accurate budget, and staying on track without overspending. This can help ensure you stay within your spending limits without incurring unnecessary expenditures.

Implement these additional tips when planning and budgeting for travel to save money while making the most of your travel experiences.

Immersing yourself in local culture

Here are some ways you can make the most of your time spent around the local culture of the country you visit:

Stay with a local: For a more authentic travel experience and insight into local culture and traditions, try booking a homestay or Airbnb with a host from your destination city. They can show you around and teach you all about daily life there!

To find a range of interesting options for staying with a local, try searching for these terms. Add the country you are visiting at the end of each one:

- *"Homestay travel"*
- *"Airbnb experiences"*
- *"Local host accommodation"*
- *"Authentic travel experiences"*
- *"Staying with locals for a more immersive travel experience"*

Attend cultural events: When travelling abroad, look out for cultural events like festivals, concerts and local performances to gain a greater appreciation for your destination's culture and traditions.

Sign up for a cooking class in your area: Cooking classes offer an engaging way to discover local cuisine and culture. Not only can you gain new cooking skills and try unique food, but you'll meet interesting locals too!

Visit local markets: Local markets offer an excellent way to immerse yourself in local culture and interact with locals, offering delicious local foods, handmade crafts and insight into their economy.

Learning the local language: Picking up some key phrases or words of the local language can be an enjoyable way to interact with locals and respect their culture, and can enrich your travel experience as well.

Useful phrases to learn when you travel anywhere:

- *"Excuse me, can you help me?"*
- *"Where is the nearest train station/bus stop?"*
- *"How much does it cost?"*
- *"Can I pay with a credit card?"*
- *"Is there a public restroom nearby?"*
- *"Can I have a menu, please?"*
- *"Do you have any vegetarian/vegan options?"*
- *"Can I get a glass of water, please?"*
- *"How do I get to (name of attraction)?"*
- *"What time does the (museum/restaurant/shop) open/close?"*
- *"Can you recommend any local specialities or must-try dishes?"*
- *"Do you speak English?"*
- *"Can I have the bill/check, please?"*
- *"Is there Wi-Fi here?"*
- *"Can you call a taxi for me?*

Utilising these additional tips in your travel experience will enable you to immerse yourself in local culture and gain a better understanding and appreciation of the destination, enriching the travel experience while making you an engaging traveller.

Develop a sense of curiosity and wonder that can enhance your appreciation for life

Exploring with an open mind and sense of wonder will enrich your travel experience and provide greater appreciation.

Here are some steps that will help foster these qualities during your travels:

Ask questions: Be inquisitive and pose questions about the culture, history, and way of life at your destination. Talk with locals to gain more insight from their perspectives on the area.

Try these:

- *"What's the history of this place?"*
- *"Can you recommend any local foods that I should try?"*
- *"What do people typically do for fun around here?"*
- *"How has this place changed over the years?"*
- *"What's the significance of this monument/building?"*
- *"Can you tell me about any festivals or celebrations that happen here?"*
- *"What are some interesting facts about this area?"*
- *"What are some hidden gems that not many tourists know about?"*
- *"Can you teach me a few phrases in the local language?"*
- *"What's the best way to get around the city?"*
- *"How do locals typically spend their weekends?"*
- *"What's the most popular tourist attraction in this area?"*
- *"Are there any local customs or traditions I should be aware of?"*
- *"Can you recommend any books or movies that are set in this location?"*

- *"What's the best time of year to visit this area?"*

Slow down and appreciate: Take some time to truly notice and appreciate the world around you, noting small details and appreciating its beauty.

Learn from others: Be open to learning from others, whether fellow travellers, locals, or tour guides. Everyone offers something special and has experiences they want to share.

Write a travel journal: Writing down your thoughts, observations, and experiences can help you reflect upon them while developing an appreciation of our world.

Prompts for your travel journal:

- What are your initial thoughts and feelings about the place you're visiting?
- Describe the scenery and landscape around you.
- What are the local people like? What customs or traditions have you noticed?
- Write about any cultural or historical sites you've visited and your impressions of them.
- Describe any local cuisine you've tried and whether you enjoyed it.
- What new experiences have you had since arriving at your destination?
- Have you encountered any challenges or obstacles during your travels? How did you overcome them?
- Write about any interesting conversations or interactions you've had with locals or other travellers.
- How has your perspective or understanding of the world changed since arriving at your destination?
- What have you learned about yourself during your travels?

- Describe any particularly memorable moments or experiences you've had.
- What are your goals for the rest of your trip?
- Write about any observations or reflections you have about the environment or sustainability ethics in the place you're visiting.
- What are you looking forward to experiencing or exploring next?
- Write about any new insights or perspectives you've gained from your travels.

Cultivating experiences in your daily life, even if you can't travel

Participate in a community garden: Joining a community garden can be an amazing way to connect with nature, learn gardening techniques, and meet like-minded individuals within your local area. Search out local community gardens, or consider starting one yourself!

Conduct a silent hike: Enjoy a peaceful, meditative walk in nature without music or conversation being played in the background, to connect more closely to both nature and yourself.

Attend a sound bath: Sound baths offer an unparalleled meditation experience in which participants lie back and listen to various instruments like gongs and singing bowls for relaxation and stress reduction. A sound bath can also help strengthen and boost overall well-being.

Make an "acts of kindness" day: Choose one day each month where you perform random acts of kindness for others, such as buying their coffee or writing them an encouraging note. This can be an uplifting way of spreading positivity and connecting with those in your community.

Attend virtual events: Many organisations and communities provide virtual events like concerts, lectures, and workshops as a great way to expand your horizons while staying at home. Search for virtual events related to your interests or try something completely new—there is sure to be something available!

Explore creative hobbies: Creativity can be an amazing way to enrich experiences in daily life and express yourself. Consider picking up one or more creative hobbies, such as painting, writing, or pottery, and finding classes or tutorials either online or locally.

Mindfulness can improve experiences and well-being: Mindfulness can be an incredible way to enrich experiences in daily life and enhance well-being. Try practising it through activities like yoga, meditation, or tai chi; classes are readily available both online and locally.

Starting a passion project: Undertaking a passion project can be a wonderful way to add experiences to your everyday life while exploring creative avenues. When selecting the project that aligns with your interests or passions—be it blogging, art creation, podcasting, etc.—consider connecting with like-minded individuals by starting one together! You might also benefit from meeting like-minded people online!

By exploring these innovative ideas, you can add new experiences to your everyday life and make it more exciting. Who knows what passions or interests await discovery along the way?

Discover how to communicate your experiences effectively to others, which can make you more interesting

Be specific: When sharing your experiences, be as detailed as possible. Instead of simply saying, *"I went on a trip,"* share details such as where, what, when, who was there, and why you went. This allows others to better visualise your journey while understanding it from your perspective.

Use descriptive language: When recounting experiences, employ descriptive language that vividly paints a vivid picture, for instance, *"It was breathtakingly beautiful looking out across the ocean at sunset."*

Include your feelings: Discussing how you felt during an experience can make your experiences more relatable and interesting to other people. Share what feelings it elicited within you during this eventful journey.

Request feedback: Seeking feedback can help you understand how others perceive your experiences as well as ways that you could improve storytelling.

Use multimedia: Utilising photos, videos, and other forms of multimedia will enable others to better visualise your experiences and understand your stories. Doing this will also increase listener engagement.

By applying these tips to your communication style, you can more effectively share your experiences and become more attractive to others. Sharing them may even encourage others to try something new themselves and expand on their experiences.

How to build a network of like-minded travellers

Building a network of like-minded travellers who share your enthusiasm for travel and adventure can be a great way to expand your experiences while making new connections.

Here are some helpful tips for building such a network:

Join travel groups and forums: There are various travel forums online where you can connect with other travellers and exchange experiences. Look online for groups that match up with your interests and participate in discussions about them.

Here are some search terms you could try:

- *"travel forums"*
- *"travel groups"*
- *"backpacker forums"*
- *"solo travel forums"*
- *"adventure travel groups"*
- *"family travel groups"*
- *"budget travel forums"*
- *"cultural travel groups"*
- *"foodie travel forums"*
- *"eco-travel groups"*

Attend travel events: When looking for travel opportunities in your area, conferences or expos may provide an ideal chance to meet other travellers and discover exciting new travel possibilities. These can also provide the chance to network with others while discovering more travel possibilities!

Take group tours: Group tours can be an engaging and social way to travel and make new acquaintances. When searching for tours that align with your interests or destinations you have wanted to see, keep an eye out for group tours that share them.

Create a travel-themed event: Arrange for a travel-themed potluck or slideshow party and invite those who share your passion for travel to share their own travel stories and memories.

Building a network of travel enthusiasts who share your enthusiasm can enhance your experiences and open doors to new destinations or travel styles that you hadn't considered previously. Your network may also inspire you to try things you hadn't even considered before!

In summary, by trying out these travel ideas, you can maximise your experiences and create unforgettable memories. Remember to stay open-minded as you and embrace local cultures to fully immerse yourself in your destination.

9

Finding Your Voice
HOW TO DISCOVER YOUR UNIQUE PERSPECTIVE AND STAND OUT FROM THE CROWD

Are you having difficulty communicating your ideas and opinions with confidence? Now is the time to find your distinct perspective and differentiate yourself from the competition.

In this chapter, we'll explore the importance of finding your voice for both personal and professional development. You will learn practical methods for recognising your values, beliefs and passions as well as ways to express them authentically and confidently.

I will dispel common myths about speaking up, as well as answer any of your queries on finding your voice. You'll leave with skills for effectively communicating ideas while learning how to capitalise on your unique perspective to make an impactful difference in society.

Finding your voice means more than being heard; it means being interesting to others. By mastering challenges and setbacks in expressing yourself through speech, you can develop a compelling speaking voice that garners respect from listeners.

Do not let your voice remain unheard.

Now is the time to discover and express your unique viewpoint and stand out from the pack.

Let's start now.

Most common questions and answers about finding your voice

Here are the answers to some of the most frequently asked questions about finding their voice:

Q: What does "find your voice" actually mean?

A: Finding your voice means discovering and expressing the unique perspectives, values, and beliefs that define who you are authentically and confidently.

Q: Why is finding your voice important?

A: Discovering your voice is vital because it allows you to effectively express your ideas, stand out from the crowd and make a real impactful statement about who you are in the world.

Q: How can I know if I have found my voice?

A: You will know you have found your voice when you can express your ideas and opinions with authority and authenticity, feeling empowered when speaking out, as well as an increased sense of purpose and passion from speaking up.

Q: How can I identify my values, beliefs and passions?

A: One way of discovering your values, beliefs and passions is to reflect upon past experiences, evaluate what's important to you personally and pay attention to what brings happiness and fulfilment in life.

Q: How can I speak out while it is normal to feel intimidated when speaking up?

A: We must push past any fear we feel when speaking up and express ourselves anyway. Start small by sharing your ideas with trusted colleagues or friends before expanding to larger audiences or public speaking events.

Q: How can I develop a strong speaking voice?

A: You can develop a powerful speaking voice by practising speaking aloud, using proper breathing techniques, and emphasising clarity and enunciation when practising public speaking.

Myths and truths about finding your voice

Myth: Finding your voice means being loud and aggressive

Truth: Expressing yourself authentically and confidently is the core concept behind finding one's voice; not being loud or confrontational in doing so.

Myth: Speaking out is always risky and should be avoided.

Truth: While speaking up can carry risks, speaking up also carries rewards - including personal and professional growth, strengthened relationships, and making a positive difference in the world.

Myth: It's too late to find my voice

Truth: No matter your age or profession, finding your unique perspective and starting to express yourself is never too late - discovering this aspect of yourself can lead to personal and professional fulfilment and make a powerful statement about who you are as an individual.

The importance of speaking up

Speaking out is crucial for many reasons, including building self-esteem and confidence. By asserting yourself and sharing your ideas, opinions, and values you're showing that your thoughts and feelings matter - this can increase feelings of worth and respect for oneself which in turn improve confidence levels.

Confidence makes you more attractive to others. People naturally gravitate toward people who appear self-assured and assertive; by speaking up and expressing yourself confidently, you become a people magnet who attracts those that share similar interests to yourself and can connect on deeper levels through meaningful relationships that align with values and interests that reflect on you.

Speaking out can also help overcome shyness or social anxiety. By practising speaking up and asserting yourself in social settings, over time your confidence can grow, leading to more opportunities for personal and professional growth, leading to an ultimately more fulfilling life overall.

How to express yourself confidently

Here are a few steps you can take to express yourself more confidently:

Prep in advance: If you're feeling intimidated about speaking in public, take some time to plan. Think about what you want to say and why it matters before practising saying it aloud.

Focus on your body language: Body language can convey confidence when used properly, even without words being exchanged directly between parties. Sit or stand up straight, make eye contact, and avoid fidgeting or slouching as much as possible.

Speak slowly and clearly: Mumbling or speaking too quickly may make it hard for others to comprehend you. So take your time when speaking enunciating each word.

Use "I" statements: Expressing yourself more confidently and assertively can be made easier through using statements such as, *"I believe"* or *"I feel."* Using this type of language helps people express themselves more boldly.

Never apologise for your opinions: Don't apologise for expressing your thoughts and beliefs; rather, express them boldly and politely.

Be open to feedback: Being open to feedback can help you develop both communication skills and confidence. Listen carefully to what others are telling you and use that input to refine your approach in the future.

Practice makes perfect: Confidence can only come through practice. As you express yourself more frequently and develop the strength to express it confidently over time, your confidence will grow with every repetition.

The importance of finding your voice in personal and professional development

Understanding the significance of finding your voice is paramount to personal and professional success. Being able to express yourself authentically and with conviction allows you to connect more closely with people, build stronger relationships, and achieve your goals more easily.

Personal development experts understand the value of finding one's voice as part of self-improvement: discovering values, beliefs, and passions help identify ways of living that align with authentic selves - providing greater purpose and fulfilment in life.

When it comes to professional development, finding your voice can make all the difference in advancing your career and positively affecting your organisation. By assertively and confidently voicing your ideas and opinions, you could become a thought leader and influencer within your field.

Practical techniques for identifying your values, beliefs, and passions

Here are a few practical techniques you can use to identify your values, beliefs and passions:

Reflect on your experiences: Recall those events which have had the greatest meaning in your life; which values or beliefs they encapsulated or passions they inspired within you.

Imagine your heroes: Think about who inspires you the most and think about their values, beliefs and passions that could serve as models in your own life. How could these traits be integrated into the way that you lead it?

Recognise your strengths: Take time to identify what skills or activities come naturally to you or that interest you most, and how these relate to your values, beliefs, and passions.

Conduct a values evaluation: With so many online values assessments available today, taking one of them and reflecting upon the results can help identify your core values and help shape your life decisions.

Keep a journal: Document your experiences, beliefs and values as you relate to each. Over time you may see patterns emerge which help identify passions and values that resonate within yourself.

Once you've identified your values, beliefs and passions, take steps to incorporate them into your daily life. This could include volunteering for a cause close to your heart or taking up an interest that aligns with them.

Utilising these practical techniques, you can gain a better understanding of your values, beliefs and passions - helping you live a more authentic and satisfying life as well as express yourself more freely and confidently.

How to stand out and make a difference with what you have to say

Leveraging your unique perspective is an effective way to distinguish yourself and make an impactful statement.

Here are some steps you can take to take advantage of your unique perspective:

Recognise your unique perspective: Appreciate that every perspective is valuable and different, embrace individuality and don't be afraid to express yourself authentically.

Recognise your strengths: Acknowledging what sets you apart - be it skills, experiences or personality traits - is key to taking advantage of them in your personal and professional life. Focus on taking full advantage of them!

Unleash your potential: Recognise an area or topic where your unique perspective can make an impactful statement about its importance - for example, a cause you care deeply about, an industry or community in which you reside or an association you belong to.

Share your experience: Sharing the details of your personal history can help others relate to and understand your unique viewpoint.

Network with like-minded individuals: Connecting with people who share similar passions and interests can help build a community of support while working on projects that make a difference.

Speak up and take action: Don't be intimidated to voice your ideas and opinions, then take steps to make a difference in your community or industry.

Utilising your unique perspective is one way you can stand out and make an impactful contribution to society. Don't be afraid to embrace your individuality and share it with those around you; who knows what kind of impact this could have!

Gain the confidence to share your voice in personal and professional settings

Acquiring the courage to assert yourself in personal and professional settings takes practice and hard work, here are a few steps you can take to strengthen your voice:

Plan: If speaking up is daunting for you, set aside some time in advance to prepare. Think through what you wish to convey and why it matters before practising saying your speech aloud.

Start small: To get comfortable expressing your ideas and opinions in front of an audience, start small. As your confidence builds up, increase the size and scope of your target group gradually.

Focus on your strengths: Recognising what sets you apart can help build up confidence when communicating. So identifying and exploiting those attributes which define who you are can give you a great advantage when communicating.

Do not fear failure: Don't be discouraged when making mistakes or experiencing setbacks; use failure as an opportunity to gain new insights that will enable you to improve your approach going forward.

Seek out support: Making connections with those who believe in your efforts can help build your confidence and hone your voice. This may enable you to develop it further.

Utilise self-care: Make time to care for yourself both physically and mentally by practising activities like exercise, meditation or journaling that promote resilience and confidence.

How to navigate challenges and setbacks when expressing your voice

Be receptive to feedback: When receiving criticism on your ideas or communication style, view it as an opportunity to grow as an individual.

Stay true to your values: In times of challenge or setback, we must remain true to ourselves and our beliefs. Don't compromise your integrity for others' approval.

Be flexible: Be open to adapting your approach as necessary when communicating, which can help you navigate different people and situations more easily.

Active listening: When communicating with others, practice active listening by paying close attention to what they are saying and validating their perspectives. Doing this will enable you to strengthen relationships while more efficiently confronting challenges.

Utilise positive self-talk: When faced with challenges or setbacks, use positive self-talk as a means to keep yourself motivated and resilient. Remind yourself of all of your strengths and accomplishments to remain optimistic.

Reach out: When faced with challenges or setbacks, seek support from trusted friends, mentors or colleagues. Sometimes just talking through an issue can provide invaluable insights and perspectives that could make life simpler.

By employing these strategies, you can more effectively navigate challenges and setbacks when expressing your voice. Don't forget that self-expression takes time and practice - setbacks are inevitable along the way! With perseverance and effort, however, you can overcome challenges to make a positive contribution with your voice to society.

Start finding your voice today by reflecting on your values, beliefs and passions - such as what motivates and matters deeply to you. Once identified, begin sharing your opinions through conversations with friends or coworkers in small ways.

As you become more at ease expressing yourself, gradually expand the scope of your audience by speaking up in team meetings or posting ideas on social media. The more often you find your voice, the more engaging and compelling it will become for others.

10

The Power Of Embracing Challenges
HOW TO OVERCOME ADVERSITY AND BECOME UNFORGETTABLE

Life can present many obstacles and it can seem easier to avoid them entirely, but accepting challenges can be one of the most effective strategies for achieving growth and success.

In this chapter, we will examine the power of accepting challenges as it leads to overcoming adversity and creating unforgettable moments in our lives.

Many individuals may have questions regarding why and how they should embrace challenges, along with any benefits that they might expect from doing so. Here I will answer these questions as well as dispel common myths related to venturing outside our comfort zones.

By learning to embrace challenges, you can develop resilience and coping skills that will benefit you throughout your personal and professional lives. You'll discover ways to reframe challenges as opportunities for growth and learning - creating a growth mindset that embraces experimentation and risk-taking.

This chapter will also teach you how to effectively communicate your unique strengths and values by drawing from your experience of overcoming challenges.

So whether you are facing difficult circumstances now or simply wish to develop the skills needed to face future obstacles, this chapter offers practical techniques and inspiration that will enable you to embrace challenges head-on and grow from them.

Time to start embracing those challenges!

Most common questions and answers about embracing challenges

Q: Why should I embrace challenges?

A: Challenging yourself can help you grow and discover new skills, while at the same time providing a sense of achievement and strengthening confidence. Stepping outside your comfort zone may reveal uncharted territory of personal and professional advancement.

Q: How can I develop resilience and coping abilities?

A: There are various techniques for developing resilience and coping skills, including mindfulness meditation, cognitive-behavioural therapy and physical exercise. Finding one that suits your lifestyle best should become part of your routine.

Q: How can I transform challenges into opportunities for personal growth and learning?

A: One way to reframe challenges is to view them as opportunities to develop new skills and knowledge, build relationships, or reduce feelings of stress and anxiety. Focusing on the potential benefits can help alleviate feelings of tension.

Q: How can I present and articulate my unique skills and values?

A: One approach to communicating your unique strengths and values is through storytelling techniques such as telling personal accounts of how you have overcome challenges. Doing this allows people to see your resilience, determination, unique perspective on life etc. As part of this exercise, you may also use storytelling techniques to make these experiences even more engaging and memorable for them.

Q: How can I develop a growth mindset that accepts experimentation and risk-taking?

A: One way to cultivate a growth mindset is by prioritising learning over achieving specific results. You could try viewing mistakes and failures as opportunities for personal growth and improvement. Furthermore, practising mindfulness helps keep us present and open to new experiences.

Q: How can embracing challenges help me stand out?

A: Involve yourself with challenges to develop an individual perspective that stands out from others and shows resilience, determination and the ability to adapt to any changing circumstance. These traits may make you attractive to potential employers or collaborators while creating a powerful personal brand for yourself.

Q: How can I use my experience overcoming obstacles to reach my goals?

A: One way you can apply your experience of overcoming challenges is by setting specific goals and devising an action plan to reach them. Lean on previous successes to boost confidence and motivation while identifying the skills and resources needed to meet current objectives. Furthermore, seek mentors or role models who have successfully navigated similar trials to learn from their experiences.

Myths and truths regarding embracing challenges

Myth: Failure is something to avoid at all costs.

Truth: Adopting an attitude of openness toward failure allows for risk-taking and exploration - perhaps leading to new opportunities and success!

Myth: Only certain individuals can overcome challenges.

Truth: Anyone can develop the mindset and skills necessary to conquer challenges head-on and thrive during challenging situations; all it takes is cultivating a growth mindset and building resilience through practice and experience.

Myth: Challenges are always negative and should be avoided.

Truth: Obstacles present opportunities for personal growth and learning. By viewing obstacles as positive experiences, you can lessen feelings of stress and anxiety while approaching difficult situations with more positive and proactive attitudes.

Myth: Success depends solely on natural talent or ability.

Truth: While innate talent may play an important role, success usually stems from hard work, perseverance and the willingness to take risks and embrace challenges. By cultivating a growth mindset and building resilience you can develop the necessary skills and habits necessary to achieve your goals.

Myth: Engaging with challenges is dangerous and should be avoided.

Truth: While engaging with challenges may be risky, they also present new opportunities and experiences that can enhance both your personal and professional lives. By accepting calculated risks while learning from any failures that may occur, resilience will develop along with greater success in both areas.

Gaining confidence in your ability to tackle difficult situations

Here is a step-by-step guide on how to build confidence in yourself and embrace challenging situations:

Determine the cause: Once you know which situation is causing stress or anxiety for you, begin by pinpointing its specifics - for instance a difficult project at work, conflict with colleagues, or personal challenges that need overcoming.

Deconstruct: Break down your situation into smaller, more manageable steps to help feel less overwhelmed and gain control of it all.

Assign achievable goals: Create realistic yet obtainable goals at each step in the process to stay motivated and build momentum as you make progress toward your ultimate goal.

Visualise success: Visualising yourself completing each step in the process and reaching your ultimate goal is a great way to boost confidence and alleviate anxiety. This visualisation process can also help build strength.

Practice: To cope effectively with difficult situations, practise your skills and techniques for handling them by role-playing conversations, rehearsing presentations or practising stress reduction techniques.

Reach out: When seeking support from friends, family, or colleagues it can help to seek advice, feedback or encouragement from someone trusted.

Recall past successes: Recalling past achievements can help build confidence and remind us of our ability to overcome challenges.

Here are some real-world examples of applying these steps:

Example: Imagine you have an upcoming presentation at work that you are nervous about.

To take control of it and achieve success, break it into steps - such as outlining, practising delivery and creating visual aids - with achievable goals set at each step to visualise yourself giving a successful speech.

Also, practise presentation skills while seeking feedback from colleagues. As you do so, remember past successes you had giving presentations.

Example: Imagine you are having an uncomfortable conversation with one of your close friends or family members.

Take control by breaking down conversations into smaller steps, such as identifying an issue, practising active listening and expressing your feelings and needs. Set achievable goals for each step of the process while visualising its successful completion.

Develop your communication skills further while seeking support from friends or therapists who have had similar successes resolving conflicts with others. Finally, reflect upon past victories you've had in resolving conflicts with others.

11

The Power Of Networking
HOW TO BUILD LASTING RELATIONSHIPS

Have you heard the expression, *"It's not what you know, it's who you know"?* While knowledge and skills certainly matter when it comes to professional success, networking remains essential in building meaningful relationships in today's competitive landscape. Forming meaningful bonds with others through networking is integral for reaching goals while forging meaningful connections within society.

In this chapter, we will explore the benefits of networking, dispel myths associated with it, and I will offer practical techniques for forging long-lasting relationships. Additionally, we will discover the significance of connecting meaningfully with others, including its effect on your confidence and reputation.

"What exactly is networking, and how do I start?" That's a great question and one that will be covered extensively in this chapter. We will cover many of these frequently asked questions as well as gain insight into the psychology of networking, including making a good first impression and effectively conveying your personal brand and value proposition.

Networking is more than simply exchanging business cards - it's about building relationships and becoming an essential and trustworthy member of your community.

No matter your personality type, networking is a skill that can be learned and refined. By the end of this chapter, you will have all of the knowledge and tools needed to form an empowering support network that will help ensure your success in life's endeavours.

Most common questions and answers regarding networking

Q: What is networking, and why is it essential?

A: Networking refers to the act of cultivating relationships with individuals who may provide opportunities, support and resources that may contribute to personal and professional success. Networking gives you an invaluable chance to form connections with others while learning from their experiences while creating opportunities for yourself.

Q: Do I need to be outgoing and extroverted to network effectively?

A: No. Networking is a skill anyone can develop regardless of personality type; introverts can just as effectively network as extroverts by drawing upon their strengths such as listening and observing and seeking opportunities that align with their preferences and interests.

Q: How can I begin building my network?

A: Start by identifying your goals and the people who can help you meet them. Attend events and join groups related to your interests and industry, making an effort to connect authentically and meaningfully. Social media platforms, like LinkedIn, can also be great platforms for building networks.

Q: How can I leave an indelible mark when networking?

A: Be authentic, curious, and engaging when networking. Show interest by actively listening and asking thoughtful questions of others to show that you care about their well-being and find ways to add value to discussions. Furthermore, make sure that after any event or meeting ends you follow up with people to strengthen the connections you've made.

Q: How can I network effectively despite having little experience or connections?

A: Start by identifying your goals and the people who can assist in reaching them. Attend events and join groups related to your interests and industry; strive to connect authentically and meaningfully with people; consider offering help for others' endeavours if it could strengthen trust and establish credibility.

Q: How can I build and nurture my network over time?

A: Stay in contact with your contacts by sending personalised emails or messages, sharing relevant resources or content, and finding ways to add value to their lives. Make an effort to show genuine interest in their successes and challenges as well as provide support when needed.

Q: How can I overcome my fear of networking and socialising with strangers?

A: Begin by attending smaller, more intimate events or joining groups with shared interests. Practise active listening and asking thoughtful questions while remembering that most people welcome meeting new people and building relationships. Once comfortable, gradually increase participation at larger events with a more diverse membership.

Q: How can I network effectively in a virtual or remote environment?

A: Take advantage of virtual networking opportunities, like online events and social media platforms. Be proactive in reaching out to those you wish to connect with and look for ways you can add value by providing useful resources or making introductions between contacts in your network.

Q: How can I leverage my network to find opportunities?

A: Be clear about your goals and the types of opportunities you are seeking and communicate that information with your contacts. Make an effort to stay top-of-mind by regularly sharing updates about yourself as well as finding ways to add value. Remember to reciprocate any help or support given from within your network.

Myths and truths about the art of networking

There are various myths associated with networking that can prevent individuals from building their networks successfully.

Here are a few common ones, along with their truths:

Myth: Networking involves exchanging business cards and making superficial connections.

Truth: Networking is about developing meaningful relationships with those who can offer opportunities, support, and resources that benefit all parties involved. It goes far beyond handing out business cards; networking should create meaningful bonds while adding value for those around us.

Myth: Only extroverts can network successfully.

Truth: Networking is a skill anyone can develop regardless of personality type. Introverts are just as capable of networking effectively using their strengths like listening and observing to find networking opportunities tailored specifically to them and their interests.

Myth: Networking is only for job hunters and salespeople.

Truth: Networking can be invaluable for anyone seeking to establish meaningful relationships and open doors in both their professional and personal life. Networking helps connect like-minded people, find mentors and advisors, and build a supportive network.

Myth: Networking requires too much time and is unworthy of effort.

Truth: Networking may take up time, but it is an investment in your personal and professional success. By developing strong networks you can gain access to new opportunities, gain knowledge from others and foster a sense of community within yourself and belonging.

Myth: Networking is an event-driven activity.

Truth: Networking is an ongoing process of cultivating and maintaining relationships over time. It goes beyond simply attending events or meeting people once; networking requires active engagement over time to build and nurture meaningful connections and add value to others' lives. A strong network requires consistent effort and attention.

Building a powerful network is crucial to both personal and professional success, starting with connecting meaningfully with others in an engaging manner. One method for accomplishing this is altruism - or practising selflessness toward others rather than only seeking personal gain - when approaching networking from this angle, rather than only looking out for yourself, you create positive impressions with others while building trust over time, which in turn boosts confidence levels and establishes you as an essential member of your community.

Understanding the importance of networking for personal and professional success is vitally important. With so much relying on personal connections, referrals, and word-of-mouth recommendations in today's environment, building a strong network of people who know, like and trust you is vital to increase chances of new opportunities, gain insights, and knowledge, and create a sense of community and support.

So how can you build a strong network and form meaningful connections with others? Identify your goals and the people who can assist in meeting them, attend events and join groups related to your interests and industry, and make an effort to connect authentically and meaningfully, while remembering to approach networking from a place of giving rather than receiving.

Try this:

Approach networking from a position of generosity rather than selfishness. Be generous with your time, expertise and resources and look for ways to support others' endeavours by making introductions or providing relevant resources or information - this builds trust and credibility while leaving a positive impression of yourself on others.

Maintaining and strengthening your network over time is another essential aspect of creating a powerful one.

This involves staying in contact with contacts, sharing relevant resources or information, and finding ways to add value to their lives.

Try this:

Reconnect with your contacts regularly: Set yourself a reminder every few months or so to check in with each contact. Send them a personalised email or SMS, asking about current projects or interests while sharing any updates of your own or discussing any upcoming plans or news you may have.

Share helpful resources or information: When you come across an article, blog post, or podcast you feel would benefit a contact, share it. Doing this demonstrates your thoughtfulness while adding value to their lives.

Search for ways to add value: Discover ways that can assist and support your contacts in their endeavours, such as making introductions or offering feedback on projects they may be working on.

Attend events or activities together: If there's an event or activity you think would be of mutual interest to both of you, invite them along. It will strengthen the bond between you and further network them together.

Furthermore, being open to new opportunities and experiences as well as helping and supporting others' endeavours is also key in building an effective network.

Developing the skills to communicate your personal brand and value proposition

Communication of your personal brand and value proposition can make you a more interesting and valuable person in both personal and professional environments. Your brand encapsulates all your strengths, skills, experiences, and abilities while your value proposition refers to what benefits are offered such as expertise, knowledge or network membership.

For optimal communication of your personal brand and value proposition, start by defining it. This should involve identifying any special strengths, values or experiences that make you distinct from others. When crafting your elevator pitch - a brief yet engaging speech about who you are, what you do and the value you offer - this will allow you to showcase both.

Stories can help make you more engaging by depicting your experiences, achievements and skills in an entertaining and captivating fashion. Additionally, by sharing your expertise through blog posts, articles or videos you can establish yourself as an authoritative figure within your field - making yourself more interesting and valuable to others.

Utilising social media platforms, like LinkedIn, can be an effective way of conveying your personal brand and value proposition. Using your profile to exhibit your skills and experiences, share content pertinent to your industry, and connect with peers within it can help build an impressive online presence and establish you as an asset within the community.

Overall, developing the skills to effectively convey your personal brand and value proposition can make you more engaging and valuable to others. By sharing your strengths, experiences, and expertise engagingly and memorably, you can build strong networks while opening doors to opportunities in all aspects of life.

How to leverage your network to create opportunities

Be strategic: When seeking to generate new opportunities, be strategic about who and how you approach people. Consider what benefits can be provided in exchange for their participation; create win-win situations whenever possible.

One way to create a win-win situation is to consider what benefits you can offer them in exchange for their participation. Here's an example message/email you could use:

Dear [Name],
I hope this message finds you well. I have been following your work and am impressed by your expertise in [industry/field/topic].

Therefore, I believe there may be an opportunity for us to collaborate and create a win-win scenario.

I'm currently working on a project related to [briefly describe your goal]. Your experience in [specific skill or area] would make your participation extremely valuable, and in exchange, I would offer some form of compensation (i.e. sharing your work with my network or giving feedback on one of theirs].

Please let me know if this is something you would be open to exploring further and I look forward to hearing back from you.

Best regards,
(your name here)

Be proactive: Be active in seeking opportunities. Don't sit around waiting for them to present themselves; seek them out actively by asking your network for referrals or introductions and remaining aware of industry news and trends.

Here are examples of posts and emails that you should make available on social media and email as a proactive measure to look out for opportunities:

Social Media Post:

"Excited to keep up with industry trends and seek out new opportunities! Always looking to form new relationships in [industry/field/topic]. Let's connect and see how we can support each other!"

Email Subject Line: [Re: Finding Opportunities in [Industry/Field/Topic]]

Dear [Name],

I hope that this email finds you well. I'm writing because I'm searching for opportunities in [industry/field/topic], and am wondering if any referrals or introductions could help me in my search.

I am passionate about [briefly describe your interests and goals in the industry/field/topic] and am always eager to connect with those who share this interest. If anyone knows anyone looking for someone with my skills and experience, I would greatly appreciate any assistance you could provide by making an introduction.

Thank you so much for taking the time and consideration in responding. I look forward to hearing back from you.

Kind regards,
[Your name here]

By strategically using your network, you can open up new opportunities, gain invaluable insights and knowledge, and form an empowering group that can assist with reaching your goals.

The psychology of networking - how to make a memorable impression

Networking is an intricate social process involving building genuine relationships with others. According to psychological theory, networking goes beyond exchanging business cards or making small talk; rather, it involves forging genuine bonds that help achieve your personal and professional goals. To be effective at networking it is necessary to understand the psychological factors influencing the process.

Trust is key when building strong connections. People tend to form deeper ties with those they trust and feel comfortable around, which means creating genuine relationships is essential if you wish to leave an impactful lasting impression and form strong ties with people.

To foster genuine relationships that create long-lasting impressions, use these tips:

Trustworthiness: Being yourself and being genuine are both key components to building trust with people. Be genuine when speaking about yourself to avoid misleading anyone about who you truly are or trying to portray someone else instead of yourself. Share who you are rather than pretending someone else exists.

Demonstrate interest: Show genuine curiosity for those you meet by asking questions and actively listening to their responses, demonstrating your care and willingness to form lasting relationships.

Be reliable: Building trust begins with being reliable. Keep your commitments and remain consistent in your actions to show that you can be counted upon as someone trustworthy and dependable.

Transparency is key when building trust with others, so be open and honest in all communications with others; don't withhold information or act dishonestly.

Be kind: Treat others with consideration and kindness. Show appreciation for their time and efforts while avoiding negative or critical remarks.

Employ empathy: Empathy is another key component of networking. Empathy refers to understanding and sharing others' emotions, so when you show that you care for another individual and are open to listening and understanding their perspective. Doing this builds trust and rapport and enables strong connections to form.

Body language: Positive body language can also play an integral part in networking. Your body language conveys so much information about your mood and interest in conversations - eye contact, smiling and nodding are great ways to show that you're engaged and interested, helping create bonds between individuals.

Here are some ways you can adopt positive body language:

Nod: Nodding can be an effective way of showing that you are actively listening and engaged with the conversation, encouraging the other person to continue speaking while building an emotional bond between both of you.

Body posture: An open body posture conveys much about your mood and intentions. Holding your arms uncrossed while facing another person shows that you are willing to communicate freely and are engaged in their conversation.

Lean in: By leaning slightly forward during conversations, leaning in can indicate your interest and establish closer bonds between yourself and other participants.

As part of networking, it's also crucial that you stand out positively. People remember those who make a first impression through unique experiences, skills, or perspectives; when sharing these stories and adding value through dialogue you are more likely to leave an enduring memory that can help foster long-term connections and help develop lasting connections with potential business contacts.

How to be unforgettable

Networking can help you become memorable by developing a reputation in the community as someone valuable and trustworthy.

Here are some ideas and tips to make you stand out and become the go-to person:

Be generous: Generosity is key to building meaningful relationships. Be generous with your time, resources and expertise by sharing what knowledge and experience you possess and offering assistance when possible.

Be proactive: Don't wait for opportunities to come knocking - go out there and seek them!

Being an excellent listener: Listening is key to building relationships. Take the time to listen attentively and understand others' needs and interests to build trust and establish rapport with them.

Share your passions: Sharing your interests can help connect you with people who share similar ones and build deeper, more meaningful relationships.

Stay reliable: Staying true to your word and fulfilling all commitments is key to building trust within your community. Be on time, meet all commitments made, and be reliable - these all go a long way toward creating an excellent image for yourself!

Focus on quality over quantity: Relationships matter more than numbers do - focus on building meaningful, authentic connections with those you meet than adding names to your network.

Use social media strategically: Social media can be an incredibly effective tool for networking and growing your reputation. Use it wisely to showcase your expertise, build connections with others and remain top of mind with clients.

Here are a few social media tips you can start implementing immediately to take full advantage of social media as a networking strategy:

Sharing industry news and trends: Sharing news and trends related to your industry can position you as a thought leader and keep you top-of-mind with followers.

Your knowledge will build credibility: Sharing your expertise can help establish credibility and bolster your status as an authority in your field.

Engage with others: Engage with those in your network by commenting and sharing their posts - this can help build relationships while keeping you top of mind!

Share valuable content: By offering valuable articles and blog posts relevant to your target audience, such as blog posts or infographics, you can position yourself as an invaluable resource and boost your reputation.

Stay regular: Post regularly and consistently on social media to remain at the forefront of people's minds and stay in front of your target audience.

Make use of hashtags: Utilising relevant hashtags will allow your content to be found by new viewers and help expand its reach.

Participate in Twitter chats and LinkedIn groups: Engaging in industry-related Twitter chats and LinkedIn groups can help you meet new people and expand your network.

By employing these tips, you can use social media strategically to demonstrate your expertise, build connections with others and remain top-of-mind with clients - helping to build your reputation, expand your network, and open up new opportunities.

12

A-Z Glossary Of Terms

A - Authenticity: Being genuine with oneself makes one more approachable and appealing to others.

B - Boldness: Being bold enough to take risks and try new experiences can lead to unexpected discoveries and stories that lead to exciting memories and tales of discovery.

C - Creativity: Thinking outside the box and expressing oneself in original and imaginative ways that captivate and engage others can lead to remarkable creativity.

D - Dynamism: Showing enthusiasm and energy in one's actions and interactions to increase both charm and charismatic qualities.

E - Empathy: Understanding and empathising with others' emotions and perspectives to form deeper connections and dialogues.

F - Flexibility: Being adaptable and open-minded will make you more interesting and versatile in different situations.

G - Growth mindset: Believing in one's ability for personal and professional growth and development can bring about engaging experiences and personal progression.

H - Humour: Humour can help people connect with you more closely and make them laugh, which makes you more engaging and endearing to other people.

I - Individuality: By accepting our unique qualities and expressing them authentically, we can distinguish ourselves and become more interesting individuals.

J - Joyfulness: Exhibiting an upbeat and friendly disposition will make you more approachable to others and interesting for conversation.

K - Knowledge: Being well-informed on various subjects is invaluable when engaging in meaningful dialogue and developing innovative perspectives.

L - Listening: Actively listening and taking an interest in others' experiences and perspectives can build lasting connections and make you more interesting.

M - Mindfulness: Being present and aware of one's thoughts and emotions in each moment can lead to profound insights and self-exploration.

N - Networking: Establishing relationships and connections with others that could open doors to exciting experiences and new opportunities.

O - Open-mindedness: Being open-minded means being accepting of new ideas and perspectives that could open the way to powerful experiences that transform you personally and professionally.

P - Passion: Pursuing one's passions and interests can open up many exciting experiences and new vistas of perspectives.

Q - Questioning: Posing thoughtful and intriguing queries, which can spark interesting dialogues and offer fresh perspectives.

R - Resilience: Overcoming setbacks and challenges is what defines resilience; being resilient allows one to remain more engaging and inspiring as an individual.

S - Storytelling: Telling engaging and captivating tales to create more engaging interactions and lasting impressions with those around you.

T - Travel: Exploring different cultures and environments can lead to unique experiences that help foster personal development and growth.

U - Uniqueness: Recognising and celebrating one's individual qualities can set one apart and make them more interesting, making life more fascinating for themselves and their fellow human being.

V - Versatility: Being adaptable and versatile can make you more interesting and capable in various circumstances.

W - Wisdom: Acquiring invaluable life experience-based wisdom can make one, even more, interesting and inspiring.

X - X factor: Being known for something exceptional or captivating that sets them apart can make for more captivating and unforgettable stories and events in our lives."

Y - Young curiosity: Foster a sense of curiosity and wonderment which can lead to exciting experiences and breakthroughs.

Z - Zeal: Showing enthusiasm for one's activities can make you more attractive and inspiring to others.

www.ingramcontent.com/pod-product-compliance
Lightning Source LLC
Chambersburg PA
CBHW050232120526
44590CB00016B/2060